Robert P. Dick

Hebrew Poetry

Robert P. Dick
Hebrew Poetry
ISBN/EAN: 9783337317089

Printed in Europe, USA, Canada, Australia, Japan

Cover: Foto ©Thomas Meinert / pixelio.de

More available books at **www.hansebooks.com**

HEBREW POETRY.

Sunday Afternoon Lectures

BEFORE

THE GREENSBORO LAW SCHOOL,

BY

Hon. ROBERT P. DICK,
U. S. District Judge.

GREENSBORO:
C. F. Thomas, Book and Job Printer.
1883.

LECTURE I.

THE INFLUENCE OF POETRY ON NATIONAL DEVELOPMENT.
THE INFLUENCE OF THE BIBLE ON MODERN CIVILIZATION.

Poetry is an interesting and instructive part of a nation's history, as it is a production of the intellectual and moral faculties, feelings and sentiments of the people.

These faculties, feelings and sentiments are awakened and intensified, in a great degree, by the spectacles of natural beauty and usefulness presented in the earth, seas and skies, which are produced by the wondrous combinations of physical laws and agencies everywhere evidencing a wisdom, power and goodness, higher, purer and vaster than human intellect and benevolence; and ever lifting the soul in love, adoration and praise to the great Creator and benefactor, and to the immortal life of a higher and more effulgent glory yet to come. In the poetry of a nation we can feel the pulse-throb of national life that shows its healthful development or decay.

In the history of the past we find that a poetic spirit has existed in a more eminent degree in some nations than in others; but among all the higher types of mankind—those races which have exerted a marked influence upon human progress—poetic feeling and sentiment seem to have permeated the entire mass of the population. These feelings and sentiments were imperceptibly formed by the pure aspirations, affections and emotions of man's better nature. They were the spirit-voices of the true, the beautiful and the good which rose above the jarring discords of selfishness, passion, prejudice and strife that marred the happiness and beauty of everyday life, and blended into the sweet harmonies of domestic joy and the noble amenities and gentle charities of social communion and brotherhood.

The Samian philosopher, in studying the principles of music, and observing the order, regularity and harmony with which the celestial bodies moved through the heavens, formed the beautiful conception that the spheres of different magnitudes and velocity, by striking against the ether, produced a music unheard by mortal ears, but ever swelling in glorious harmonies. Modern science, in discovering the universal power of gravitation which controls the motion of the planets as they roll in perfect harmony and beauty in the vast fields of immensity, has not entirely dispelled the old philosophic dream, and the imaginative mind still fancies that the morning stars have not ceased the song they sang at creation's dawn, when the "sons of God shouted for joy." How beautifully is this idea presented by Shakespeare in the Merchant of Venice.

" Look how the floor of heaven
Is thick inlaid with patines of bright gold.
There is not the smallest orb which thou beholdest
But in his motion like an angel sings,
Still quiring to the young-ey'd Cherubins;
Such harmony is in immortal souls,
But whilst this muddy vesture of decay
Doth grossly close it in, we cannot hear it."

Science has made us acquainted with the existence and with some of the influences of gravitation, but we know very little of the source, nature and extent of that wondrous power that pervades the universe. As this incomprehensible force regulates and controls the motions and relations of the celestial bodies, so there are mysterious and all-pervading influences which link the hearts of mankind with chords of kindred sympathies. From these interlinking and intermingling heart-chords many spontaneous thoughts, feelings and emotions of the soul sound out and blend into the sweetest harmonies of life—just as the viewless winds wake soft molodies on Æolean harp-strings. These soul harmonies give inspiration to genius. They form and color the ideal conceptions of the artist; they are heard in the music of the simple home song, the ballad of the minstrel, the enchanting opera, the sublime oritorio and the soul-thrilling anthem. The poet gives them sweet utterance in the musical elegance and pathos of the lyric, and the eloquent strains and flowing rhythm of epic verse.

In the infancy of nations, like in the time of childhood, we find the imaginative faculties more highly developed than the reasoning powers. The literary memorials of nearly every people, in their first rude stages of development—the period of national childhood—are the songs of bards which give expression to earnest and impassioned popular thought, imagination and feeling in language glowing with enthusiasm and highly wrought imagery. In the more advanced stages of progress, experiment, education and other elements of civilization produce the profound maxims and truths of science and philosophy, and teach the more practical duties and destinies of life; but the poetic feelings and sentiments which influenced earlier generations are not destroyed, as they are deeply implanted in the human heart, and they are elevated and refined by the ennobling and expanding influences of the enlightened mind; and they waken and vibrate with harmony when the mystic strings of the heart are touched by some master hand of genius.

The real and full history of a nation never has, and never can be written, as the various and minute causes and events which form and regulate national life pass away like the germs, the buds and blossoms of spring that change into the golden harvests of summer and the rich fruits of the autumn.

We see grand social and political results, and in some degree comprehend the proximate causes which produced them, but we know very little of the minute original elements which were silently and mysteriously combined to form such proximate causes. The little first elements of human development are fully known only to the Infinite Mind that mingled them together into creating and controlling powers. Thus it is in the natural world. We see some of the results of the tempest—hear the reverberating thunder and are dazzled with the gleaming lightning, but we know little of *when*, *where*, *how* and *why* were formed the cloud-chariots in which the majestic storm moves in grandeur through the darkened skies.

We see the rich landscape spread out in vernal beauty, but we are unable by any process of artistic analysis to tell with completeness and accuracy how its lights and shades and various objects were produced and skilfully blended into picturesque loveliness. We see the ever-rolling river as it moves grandly to the sea, widening and deepening as it flows, but we cannot trace its course back to the thousand springs that swell its volume as they trickle from mountain crags or with musical gladness gush from the bosom of the valleys.

Thus it is with a nation's poetry. There were thousands of humble hearts that, in poverty and obscurity, throbbed with loves, hopes, joys and fears, and, almost unconsciously, produced thoughts and fancies of the finest poetry that mingled with a nation's literature; just like the perfume of flowers mingling into a balmy atmosphere, or like tiny rippling rills swelling the currents of broad and sun-bright rivers, that flow with majestic harmony and join the sublime and ever-sounding symphonies of the seas.

We cannot tell when and how God sows the seeds of the wild flowers, that steal into bloom and perfume and embellish the earth; how with sunshine, rain drops and gentle dews, and the various agencies in His wondrous laboratory, He changes the scattered grain of the husbandman into the golden harvests; how He keeps in perennial flow the limpid fountains that supply the singing rills that keep fresh the verdure of the hillsides and the valleys; and how He teaches the joyous birds to trill their gladsome notes of melody.

God formed the earth as a beautiful home for man, and it was consecrated with His benediction and the songs of the angels. He also gave to man the faculties for perceiving and appreciating the true, the beautiful and the good, and enabled him to express his feelings and emotions of love, joy, hope and devotion in the rhythmic strains of poetry and the sweet, soft notes of melody. Poetry and music may well be considered as ministering angels which ever keep in living purity and freshness on earth some of the bliss of the sinless Eden.

The poet who said "Let me write a nation's songs, and I care not who writes its laws," was, by no means, a visionary enthusiast, but he was a profound philosopher, who, by intuition, observation and experience, had learned some of the strong influences which mould a nation's life. The songs and poems of a nation are important elements in its history, and they furnish the words, thoughts and imagery that sparkle like jewels in its language and literature.

While the Welsh Bards lived their nation was unconquerable. With rude minstrelsy they aroused the enthusiastic patriotism of that brave and imaginative people who loved liberty and the craggy mountains and wild valleys that lie between the Severn and the sea.

The simple songs which are sung in the cottages among the Hartz mountains and beside the Baltic, the Danube and the Rhine link even the self-exiled German to the memories and scenes of the Vaterland with ties of love and devotion which time and distance are powerless to break.

The *Ranz des Vaches* is indeed to the Switzer a song of home, and when heard even in the fairest climes of the earth causes tears of love to flow, and carries his heart back again to the humble cottage where his mother nursed him in the Alpine glen.

The Marseillais Hymn inspired French patriots with dauntless heroism in the early years of that grand revolution which so long filled Europe with mourning and the horrors of strife and carnage, and resulted in misery and martial glory, but not freedom to France.

"God Save the Queen" is intimately associated with England's greatness and renown, and keeps in glowing life the national love and loyalty of those brave and gallant sailors and soldiers whose *reveille* greets the rising sun as it gilds with morning light every clime of the earth.

"The Star Spangled Banner" fills every patriotic American heart with love and pride for that glorious land whose flag of stars is the emblem of freedom, and whose protection and power are co-extensive with the globe.

"Home Sweet Home" is one of the dearest and most touching domestic lyrics that human voice has ever sung, and is almost worthy of the lips of the sinless Seraphim. Its tender pathos causes the eyes to fill with tears and the bosom to swell with the holiest and purest emotions.

"Old Hundred" makes us think of brave, noble and glorious old Luther, and it is one of the grandest *te deums* that ever rose from human hearts and swelled through the aisles and arches of the earthly temples of Jehovah.

The grand events of the battlefield, the policies of rulers, and the laws of legislative assemblies form renowned epochs in a nation's history, but they furnish little knowledge of its inner life, or those secret causes which silently and surely formed and developed its destiny. If we view only the few transactions preserved by the historic muse we will not possess a more accurate idea of the peculiar characteristics of a nation than we would have of its geography and scenery by catching glimpses of the grand outlines of its country through the hazy curtain of the distance.

How little would the traveler know of Scotland by standing upon the castle of Edenboro and gazing over

> "That land of brown heath and shaggy wood,
> Land of the mountain and the flood."

He would see Holyrood surrounded by the hallowed memories of Scotland's royalty. He would see the ivy-clad ruins of old baronial castles, where Wallace, the Bruce and Douglas fought for freedom; but he would know little

> "Of those hills of glorious deeds,
> Those streams renowned in song,
> The blithesome braes and meads,
> Our hearts have loved so long."

He might see through the azure distance Ben Lomond and Ben Nevis, stern and wild, baring their rocky breasts to the storm as they had done for ages, but he would know nothing of Lock Katrine and Lock Lomond resting so placidly among the Highlands, and ever reflecting images of the beauties of nature that enchant their shores; or of the heathery hillsides where Roderick Dhu and MacGregor trod as lords, and were as free and fearless as the wild eagle of the mountains. He might see the gray Grampian and the Cheviot hills, the shimmering sunlight on the misty moorlands, the shining Forth and the lofty cliffs that mark the course of the distant Clyde, all blending into landscapes of imposing grandeur and rural beauty; but he would know nothing of the humble kirks where, with earnest hearts, a noble and hardy yeomanry meet to worship God in their father's simple faith, and where are heard the mournful requiems of the shadowing elms beneath whose quivering shades the hero martyrs of the Covenant sleep in hallowed graves.

He would know nothing of the virtue, contentment and domestic bliss of the cotter's home; or the simple joys in the hamlets on the "Banks of Doon," where the Ploughman Poet sang his matchless lays; or of the musical rills and trysting trees in the shady glens where many a Highland Mary listened to the whispered vows of love.

No one can know the history of Scotland, with all its thrilling incidents and sacred memories unless he has read her ballad minstrelsy and the matchless poems of her mighty sons of genius, who have invested her with the halo of song and old romance, made her a home of poesy, and enshrined her name in every heart that loves the true, the beautiful and the brave.

On many pages of recorded history we find some evidence of the influence of poetry in the formation of national character. The age of Homer was the commencement of Grecian glory. His transcendent genius not only gave immortality to his country, but created classic literature. His wonderful poems kindled those fires of patriotism, freedom and love of glory in his nation's heart which in after times shone so brightly in the wisdom of her philosophers and law-givers, in the matchless productions of her painters and sculptors, in the immortal tragedies, epics and songs of her poets, in the indomitable valor of her heroes and in the thrilling eloquence of her orators. His magic touch unsealed the fountains of Castalia and Hippocrene and made all the hills and vales of Greece the homes of the gods and the haunts of the Muses. Who can ever think of Greece, and forget the mighty bard who breathed the inspirations of genius into her national life. Her political power has passed away, her magnificent temples are now in ruins, the remnants of her art treasures are scattered over the civilized world, and the blood of the heroes of Marathon now flows in the veins of degenerate sons. The mournful Ægean among green isles and on rocky shores is ever murmuring a lament for the departed glory of old Hellas; but still the light of her poetry is as immortal as her starry skies and golden sunshine, and lingers around that classic land and makes it a sacred shrine to every lover of freedom, art and letters.

I will devote but a few moments in considering the history of the once proud mistress of the world and her nobly gifted sons of song. She drank deeply of the blood of carnage, revelled long amidst the spoils of conquest, and for centuries the great throbbings of her passionate heart were felt throughout the grandest empire of the ancient world. Her Catos, Scipios and Cæsars are gone. Her Emperors who wielded an iron sceptre over the world are dust and ashes. Not one stone of the capitol is left upon another. The Coliseum is still a grand and glorious ruin. Where once sounded the eloquence of the Forum and Senate Chamber is now heard the plaintive cry of the beggar; and the Campus Martius where once victorious legions trod in the martial pomp and pride of the triumph, is now covered with the homes of poverty and the dens of infamy and crime. But her poets still live and will live forever. In their day they shed an immortal glory upon their country which survived her costly palaces, stately temples and imperial power, and sent gleams of intellectual light over the whelming deluge of Vandal invasion, and materially assisted in kindling the splendid dawn of the renaisance day. During the night time of the Middle Ages the voice of song never became silent, but cheered the heart and elevated the mind of ignorant, superstitious and oppressed humanity in the nations of Western Europe. The poems of Cædmon, the Saxon, stand first on the rich pages of English literature. The songs of the Troubadours gave a cultured language and refined manners to Provence and Languedoc, and poetic literature was the pride and glory of the Oriental civilization of Southern Spain.

Dante may well be regarded as the greatest pioneer in the cause of freedom and intellectual progress, and we cannot read the history of the revival of learning in

Europe without being impressed with the important influence of his poetry, and of that of his brilliant successors, upon the progress of modern civilization.

When we turn to the pages of English history to study the causes which produced the intellectual development and advancement of our own ancestors, we find that Chaucer, Spenser, Shakespeare and Milton led the vanguard of progress, and were amongst the greatest benefactors of their race. The influence which they exerted will last as long as the English language is spoken, and will be as widespread as the rich beneficences of English institutions and literature.

In this place I cannot dwell longer upon a theme so suggestive, so extensive, so diversified and so full of important instruction; but I will now turn to Hebrew poetry and literature which will be the subject of my future lectures.

This is the richest and most beautiful field of literature and philosophy ever presented to human contemplation. It is a field in which intellectual giants have wrought, whose lips were touched with hallowed fire and whose inspired genius uttered the most momentous truths, and waked the grandest and sweetest notes of immortal harps. Here our minds can be elevated and enriched with the profoundest wisdom, and our souls be enraptured with scenes of loftiest sublimity, and with prophetic visions illumined with supernatural splendors. Here we can sometimes feel that we are beneath the shadow of the Almighty, and can almost hear the echo of the songs of the angels. Here in thought and fancy we can revisit the blissful Eden home where the fruitful trees of life by crystal rivers were growing, where the landscape was bright with golden light and emerald verdure, and the musical air was redolent with ambrosial odors from yellow meads of asphodel and from amaranthine bowers.

Hebrew literature must always be a subject of interesting study and contemplation to the human mind, for it has exerted a wonderful and controlling influence upon the intellectual, moral and social development of mankind.

Hebrew poetry is also the great fountain of living waters, whose perennial currents have irrigated the world of letters, and given life and beauty to so many of the bright and sweet flowers of genius that bloom in the rich and varied fields of human thought.

The most acute, profound and enlightened minds, after long and laborious investigation, have not been able fully to comprehend the extent of the influence of the Bible upon the happiness and progress of mankind. It reaches over the whole course of human destiny. Unlike other histories the Bible presents no fabulous ages. With the Bible as a guide, we can trace the course of human progress back through the darkness of oblivious centuries to the primal, sinless home in Eden, where God formed man in His own image and breathed into his nostrils the breath of life, and man became a living soul ; and we can go still further back to the time when in the *beginning* God created the heavens and the earth, and spoke those gloriously sublime words, "Let there be Light," heard only by the angels.

I cannot pause to consider at any length the influence of the Bible upon the civilization of the various nations of antiquity. The Old Testament scattered rays of light that penetrated the surrounding darkness and illumined the minds of ancient sages, philosophers, law-givers and poets, and threw some gleams of brilliance upon the institutions which they formed, and upon the immortal literatures which they gave to mankind. Investigations upon this subject have been made by learned men of modern times, and the results of their labors are impressive and wonderful. Even the annals of profane history and literature teach us that the Bible is the source of most of those high and noble thoughts, truths and principles which have illumined and beautified the moral and intellectual life of mankind and regulated correct human action. It has not only given religion, beneficent civil institutions and rich literatures to the nations of Christendom, but has contributed all that is elevating and valuable in the faith of Islam. It has not only affected the political destinies of States, but has permeated the whole structure of civilized society and shed its hallowing light over the loves, hopes and joys of domestic life.

I propose, in this place, very briefly to refer to the influence of the Bible upon the literature and æsthetic culture of modern times. The Bible was the principal cause of the revival of letters in Europe, and controlled the various agencies that contributed to the production of Christian civilization.

The dawn of the renaisance day was not produced by the sudden exercise of omnific power, like that which sent the light in kindling splendors over the face of chaos, but still it was tne result of the same Omnipotent direction. The dark ages were not only times of disintegration and decay, but they were also times of recreation and development, in which were commingled and combined various causes to produce grand results. The tides of Vandal barbarism that swept over the provinces of Western Europe produced great moral and intellectual darkness, but Grecian literature shone with a feeble light on the shores of the Bosphorus, and Oriental culture illumined the capitals of the Califs and the Moorish cities of Spain. These elements of civilization were largely introduced into Western Europe by the crusades, and produced a reviving and enlightening influence. As the human mind became more enlightened it was prompted to investigation and enquiry; and began to collect and concentrate the scattered rays of moral and intellectual light that existed in the surrounding gloom. There never was a complete intellectual midnight in the nations of Christendom. Mankind became greatly corrupted by the demoralizing influences of ignorance, superstition and hierarchal and feudal tyranny; the public services of Christian worship degenerated to almost pagan idolatry, but still in many a secluded valley, obscure home and lonely cloister the Bible kept alive the light of Christian truth and faith in many a pious heart, and kindled hopes and aspirations for a higher and more glorious destiny for man. These obscure homes of Christianity were pure little fountains from which trickled many tiny intellectual and moral rills, that flowed onward, like the mystic river of Ezekiel's vision, and continued to widen and deepen their currents, receiving into their bosom and purifying the streams of classic civilization until the nations were refreshed into more vigorous life and rejoiced in their combined and vivifying beneficences.

During the Middle Ages manuscript copies of the Bible were few and costly, and could be obtained only by the wealthy and great; and the policy of the Romish Church had made the Scriptures almost a sealed book to the multitude, but the poetry of old Israel dwelt in the hearts and memories of the people, and the paintings of Bible scenes, sketched by the rude limners of Christian art in the Catacombs and Churches of Mediæval Europe kept alive the ardent faith and hopes of pure Christianity.

While the winds, the earthquakes and the fires of God's retributive judgments swept over the face of Europe, the same "still small voice" that spoke to Elijah in the cave of Horeb, spoke again to many earnest and devout Christian men and sent them forth with all the zeal and energy of the old prophet to collect, cheer and comfort the scattered remnants of the spiritual Israel who would not bow the knee to Baal. During this dark period poetry and art were the principal conservators of Bible truth, which they taught to the multitude, and they were used by an All-Wise Providence as important agents in producing modern civilization. They were the herald angels of the dawn that awoke the minds and hearts of Europe with songs of joy and visions of beauty. They inspired Dante when he struck his solemn lyre and thrilled mankind with new pulses of life, and soon all the nations were filled with the sublime melodies of responsive harps. Then Giotto, with the touch of genius, gave new inspiration and beauty to Christian art which was soon illumined by the glorious light shed by Da Vinci, Raphael and Angelo.

Then music, with enchanting power, began to wake higher and sweeter strains—the prelude notes that afterwards swelled into the sublime oratorios of Handel, Mozart and Beethoven. Then the spirit of freedom, which had been entombed in the ruins of the past, began to stir the minds and hearts of men to break the chains of civil and religious bondage which had so long repressed free thought and intellectual energy. Soon the mighty influences of partially emancipated and enlightened thought exhibited their vivifying powers. The preaching of Wickliffe was heard on the banks of the Thames, like the voice of another forerunning prophet crying in the wilderness, "Prepare ye the way of the Lord, make his paths straight." The tones of this grand message rang in echoing cadences among the hills of Bohemia as Huss and Jerome were marching to the stakes of martyrdom, and a century afterwards the evangel of Luther was heard in the Church of Wittenburg, sounding like the silver trumpet of the Jubilee, proclaiming universal freedom of thought, and then the grand march of the Reformation began which conducted mankind from the darkness of the past into the ever-brightening realms of the future.

I will not so far forget the truths of history as to deny to classic learning its just claims in the intellectual regeneration of mankind, but I insist that its influence was only of secondary importance when compared with the elevating, ennobling and enlightening power of the Bible Classic learning cultivated and refined the taste and intellect; the Bible educated the mind and heart by bringing out the highest thoughts and purest emotions and sympathies of man's better nature, and elevated the soul in its aspirations for a higher and nobler life in this world and in eternity.

Classic learning has contributed to only a few of the branches of knowledge, while the Bible has poured its treasures of virtue, truth, wisdom and holiness into the whole structure of society. Even in the department of the fine arts the Bible has done more than antique models in inspiring artistic genius with those ideal conceptions of the grand and beautiful which have touched the heart and won the admiration of mankind. Most of modern sculpture was formed after antique models, while nearly all of the grandest paintings of the Old Masters were Bible scenes. The productions of the chisel are cold, colorless and lifeless; they charm the eye and cultivate the taste, but speak not to the heart, while the warm, glowing and life-like Bible pictures, around which the imagination throws a halo of sacred associations, fill the heart with high and holy emotions, give the pulses a quicker throb, make the tear drops start, and thrill the soul with the eloquent ecstacies of prayer.

I will not dwell longer, in this place, upon the influence of the Bible in producing and controlling the civilization of Christendom, but may refer to the subject again in subsequent lectures.

The Bible has a wonderful inherent power of self-preservation and protection. It has encountered and triumphed over the learning, philosophy, genius and prejudices of the most enlightened nations of the ancient world ; passed unharmed through the intensely heated furnaces of persecution ; been severely tried by the strong opposition of principalities and powers ; the blasphemous criticisms of infidels ; the irrational cavils of learned and accomplished skeptics, and the incomplete discoveries and crude theories and conjectures of modern science. Like gold, it has been purified in the fire ; like the fabled Antæus, it has been strengthened by apparent overthrow. Now enlightened science is becoming its strongest ally, and the sharp attrition of infidel intellect has been like the wheel of the lapidary polishing the diamond and bringing out its purest and brightest lustre.

All persons, who, in any age, have carefully studied the Bible, with an honest and earnest purpose of obtaining the truth, have found, like Jacob wrestling with the angel, that they have received rich intellectual treasures and consoling spiritual hopes and blessings from the Most High.

In the course of lectures which I purpose to deliver to you I will speak of some of the literary excellencies and beauties of the Bible, and of the peculiar character and genius of the people to whom it was delivered by its divine Author, with the sincere hope that my imperfect efforts may induce you to enter with earnest hearts and minds upon these rich and beautiful fields of history, philosophy and poetry.

LECTURE II.

EDUCATION, CHARACTER AND LAWS OF THE HEBREWS.

In order to understand and properly appreciate the richness and beauty of the literature of the Hebrews the student should make himself familiar with their history and language; with the geography and scenery of their country; with their laws and civil and religious institutions; with their manners and customs, and other characteristics that distinguished their peculiar national life; so that in imagination he can transport himself back to the age in which they lived and catch some of the spirit that animated them while performing their part in the great drama of civilization.

This information can, in some degree, be acquired and comprehended by a careful and devout study of the Bible, which is now the entire library of the history, literature and philosophy of that ancient and most wonderful nation of mankind. I feel sure that we lose much of the sublimity and literary beauty of the Old Testament by not being able to read it in the original tongue. But few of us can find time in the midst of our professional pursuits to acquire a critical knowledge of the peculiar structure of such a difficult, ancient and unspoken language, and we must content ourselves with the English translation, and with such imperfect information as to the spirit and genius of the original as may be derived from the treatises and commentaries of learned and accomplished Hebrew scholars.

The English Bible, if thoroughly studied, will furnish us with treasures of lofty thought and poetic imagery which will enrich our minds with the highest wisdom, and fill our hearts with pure and elevated emotions, and give us a vivid conception of the glorious beauty of Hebrew literature.

The history of the Hebrews is rich in thrilling incidents, and can be distinctly traced back through the dim and shadowy regions of the past to the genesis of the nation, and then onward through an unbroken genealogy of their ancestors to the childhood of the human race. No nation can boast of such a proud heraldry as the Hebrews, and they exerted an animating and controlling influence upon all the nations with whom they came in contact. This influence among the nations may well be compared with an ever-flowing stream, producing fertility and verdure in all lands touched by its refreshing waters.

Although the sacred records of the Hebrews have much internal evidence of their truthfulness, still they are confirmed by impartial science which translates aright the language which God has written on the surface and the strata of the earth ; by the invaluable researches of comparative philology, which proves that the whole earth was of one race and one speech ; by the crumbling monuments of Egypt, and memorials dug from the graves of buried cities; by the habits and customs of many neighboring nations which have remained unchanged for three decades of centuries ; and by the universal traditions which have come down from pre-historic ages.

The history and poetry of the Hebrews are so intimately commingled that their history glows with poetry and their poetry is full of history. Everywhere on the golden thread of narrative are strung the precious and priceless pearls and gems of poetic thought.

The book of Genesis is the only authentic account which we have of the primeval history of mankind for twenty-five hundred years. The most recent writer in the Old Testament was contemporary with Herodotus, the father of profane history. More than a thousand years intervened between Moses and Malachi, and although the sacred books of the Hebrews contain such a multiplicity of topics and variety of contents, and were the productions of various minds ; composed in different ages and under different circumstances, they exhibit a wonderful continuity of spirit, thought, style and purpose, and are evidently but parts of one book, emanating from one divine source. The Bible is an intellectual and moral phenomenon without a parallel in the world of letters. It stands in the fields of literature as a sublime original. It may be compared to the sun, which is ever shedding its inherent and unwasting warmth and brightness that fills the earth with beneficence and beauty, and kindles the twinkling radiance of planets and stars in the vast and deep bosom of immensity.

From the earliest period of their national existence the Hebrews were far in advance of surrounding nations in intellectual and moral culture.

Education occupied a prominent place in their civil and religious institutions. The fathers of families were strictly enjoined to instruct their children in the national laws, history and sacred literature. The system of education established by Moses and required by law to be observed, was general in its application, and tended to develop all the intellectual faculties and moral feelings of the nation. No child of genius was prevented by penury and neglect from drinking at the pure fountains of truth and learning. The gates of knowledge were ever open and accessible to all, and duty required every one to enter and possess the rich fruits of accumulated wisdom, and contribute to the constantly increasing store. Every one from chilhood was taught the learning of the nation and the highest and noblest duties and responsibilities of life. Thus all the intellectual and moral faculties and energies of the nation were fully developed; and the day of Hebrew civilization continued to brighten until it reached its noontide splendor in the age of Solomon ; when its light and glory was shed upon surrounding nations, and was transmitted to succeeding ages.

Under the laws and institutions of Moses the priests and Levites had no inheritance, except the cities that were appropriated to them for residences, and they were supported by tithes annually collected from the tribes. By divine direction they were set apart for religious services, and as instructors of the people. They formed a sacerdotal order, but they had no means of acquiring large estates which would give them undue influence, and they could not obtain political power by operating upon the superstitious fears of the people. They could make no united and concentrated effort to unduly control the political institutions of the State, as under the wise laws of Moses their prophetic destiny was accomplished, they were "divided in Jacob and scattered in Israel." They were made special guardians of the laws, and as their maintenance depended upon the existence and observance of the laws, self interest prompted them to oppose innovations and revolutions in the State. Thus they constituted a conservative and intelligent political element, ever active in preserving the peace and good order of society, and always contributing to the mental, moral and religious culture of the people. They occupied this important position during most of the period of the commonwealth, but in the days of Samuel many associations for a higher public education were formed, called Schools of the Prophets.

These schools were attended by the young men of Israel, where they were taught the laws and literature of their country, and were instructed in sacred music. The teachers of these high schools occupied prominent positions in all legislative assemblies, and they gave public instructions on the Sabbath and at the great national festivals. From these schools, in a subsequent age, God called most of those inspired messengers who constituted "the goodly fellowship of the prophets," and who left such a glorious literature for the Hebrews and for all mankind.

The moral, social and political character of the Hebrews has been the subject of much investigation and discussion, and I think that they have not always been treated with the fairness and liberality which have been accorded to other nations. The only history of the ancient Hebrews is contained in the Old Testament. This history is sternly truthful, and was written under the influence of divine inspiration for the purpose of guidance and instruction to the nation in its future progress, and also for the benefit of all succeeding ages. No national pride and love of country influenced the prejudices and warped the judgments of the sacred historians and induced them to unduly panegyrize their countrymen and fill their annals with the highly wrought creations of fiction and fable. Their narratives are facts and not fancies, and they are filled with important truths and not moral and social theories. They were the stern censors of national vices and not the apologists of error and crime. They wrote not for self-fame, or to stimulate national vanity and ambition, and thus win popular applause. They wished to reform and regenerate their people by showing to them the heinousness and folly of sin and disobedience to Jehovah, and point out the true paths of individual and national prosperity and glory.

In judging the character of the Hebrews by their history, we subject them to a sterner ordeal than is applied to any other nation. The historians and poets of Greece and Rome employed all the powers of their inventive faculties to win fame for themselves and to advance the glory of their nation; and their productions were filled with highly wrought eulogy and fascinating fables. Most of the events and incidents mentioned in the Iliad and Æneid are ingenious fictions, and the imagination of the poets made heroes and demigods out of rapacious and cruel chieftains. Herodotus, Thucydides and Xenophon, Livy, Sallust and Tacitus did more for the renown of Greece and Rome by the partiality and brilliancy of their fancy than was achieved by the wisdom of philosophers and statesmen, and the real exploits of generals and consuls.

In modern times we find the fame of nations and the character of races, in a great degree, dependent upon the partiality, patriotism and creative genius of historians and poets.

In instituting a comparison between the Hebrews and other nations we should not forget this important fact, that the character of one is sternly and truthfully delineated by inspired penmen, while the character of other peoples are idealized by the partial pencils of human genius.

We also do great injustice to the Hebrews by judging them according to the standard of our own times. They lived in an age of almost universal moral barbarism. They were not surrounded by nations of highly cultivated tastes, refined sensibilities and elevated sentiments, and could not, by social and commercial intercourse, receive the accumulated blessings of an advanced and rapidly expanding civilization.

To them the oracles of divine truth were obscurely communicated by types and ceremonies of worship, and the symbolic teachings of priests and prophets. Their minds and hearts were not illumined, as ours have been, by the glorious light of the Gospel, and by the numerous manifestations of a Divine Providence for eighteen hundred years. We certainly would be unjust judges if we pronounce judgment of condemnation against the Hebrews because they do not come up to the present standard of Christian enlightenment and virtue.

In forming our opinion of the character of the ancient

Hebrews our judgments are too much warped and prejudiced by supposing them to have been like the bigoted, fanatical and cruel Jews who rejected, persecuted and crucified our Saviour. We seem to forget the moral degeneracy of the race produced by centuries of dissension and discord, calamity and servitude; by the loss of the sacred symbols of the first Temple; their noble and inspiring language; the voice of prophecy and the elevated spirituality of their religious faith, and also by the corrupting influence of pagan civilization with which they were brought into more immediate contact by the extension of Persian, Grecian and Roman conquest.

The Greeks of the time when St. Paul visited Athens were not like the Greeks who fought at Marathon and Salamis. The Romans who yielded a servile submission to Alaric were wholly unlike the citizens of republican Rome who, with heroic fortitude and dauntless valor, surrounded the Capitol when they heard the tremendous tidings of Cannæ. Why should we judge the Hebrews by a different standard? Why should we reverse the order of divine judgment and visit the sins of the children upon the fathers?

If we will divest ourselves of the prejudices which have been engendered in the Christian world by the conduct of the Jews towards our Saviour, and calmly judge the ancient Hebrews by the age in which they lived, the circumstances by which they were surrounded, and the influences which they have exerted upon all subsequent times, we must come to the conclusion that the Chosen People of Jehovah were not only a great but a wonderful people.

I will now briefly refer to the influence of the civil laws of Moses in forming the character of the ancient Hebrews, and in promoting the peace and prosperity of the nation by cementing the bonds of social and political union, and thus insuring a constantly progressive civilization. The subject is worthy of a more extended notice than the limits of this lecture will allow.

When we consider the antiquity of those laws, the moral darkness of the age in which they were promulgated, the consummate ability and extensive knowledge which they display, and the vivifying influences which they have so long exerted upon the destinies of mankind, we must feel that they were the productions of supernatural genius and wisdom and are worthy of our constant study and most devout veneration.

The Hebrews were a nation pre-eminently governed by law. The books of the law not only regulated the political, social and domestic relations of the people, but were the text books of their education and culture, and penetrated and permeated their entire literature. The principles of those laws constituted an integral and important part in all historical, prophetical and poetical writings, and influenced the emotional and thought-life of the people.

It is not my purpose critically to analyze those laws and point out their various excellencies. This subject has been fully considered and elaborated with much ability by Prof. Wines in his commentaries on the Laws of the Ancient Hebrews. I will quote with approbation the concluding paragraph of the chapter on Fundamental Principles:

"Such then, as I conceive, were the great ideas and fundamental principles which lay at the basis of the Hebrew State. The unity of God, the unity of the nation, civil liberty, political equality, an elective magistracy, the sovereignty of the people, the responsibility of public officers to their constituents, a prompt, cheap and impartial administration of justice, peace and fellowship with other nations, agriculture, universal industry, the inviolability of private property, the sacredness of the family relations, the sanctity of human life, universal education, social union, a well adjusted balance of powers, and an enlightened, dignified, venerable public opinion were the vital elements of the constitution of Moses. What better basis of civil polity, what nobler maxims of political wisdom does the nineteenth century offer to our contemplation, despite its boast, of social progress and reform. The institutions founded on these maxims tower up amid the barbaric darkness and despotism of antiquity, the great beacon light of the world; diffusing the radiance of a political philosophy, full of truth and wisdom, over all the ages which have succeeded that, in which they were first promulgated to mankind."

We refer to this subject in this place only for the purpose of drawing the legitimate inference, that there must have existed a condition of high moral, social and intellectual advancement among the Hebrews after they had reached the Promised Land and become a well organized nation under the laws and institutions of Moses.

Surely there can be no better evidence of the character and condition of a people than the system of laws which they reverence and cheerfully obey; for a system of laws is always regarded as the concentrated wisdom and experience of a nation—an index of public virtue and intelligence and a standard of civilization.

With such civil and political laws and institutions we cannot be surprised that the Hebrews have bestowed such rich intellectual and moral treasures upon mankind. In this respect they have partially fulfilled the promise which God made to Abraham as the reward of his sublime faith, "In thy seed shall all the nations of the earth be blessed."

Although the nations of modern times have received such manifold blessings from the Ancient Hebrews, they do not fully recognize the fact and gratefully acknowledge the obligation they owe to that God-chosen people. The rulers, statesmen, jurists and scholars who now control the destinies of nations and advance the progress of civilization, are disposed to regard the classic nations of antiquity as the primal sources of wisdom, knowledge and refined culture, when in truth those nations only dimly reflected the intellectual light which emanated from the greater orb of truth and wisdom that shone over the land of Palestine.

A candid, intelligent and industrious enquirer after truth, when he fully examines the history, laws, institutions, moral teachings, and the learning and literature of the ancient Hebrews, and then traces the benign influences which they exerted upon other ancient nations and then upon the Gospel dispensation and upon Christian civilization, will greatly admire and venerate that people whom God chose as the depositaries of His sacred oracles and as the pioneers of human progress.

The Hebrews were indeed pioneers in the fields of moral and intellectual progress. They possessed a literature abounding in the enlightened principles of jurisprudence and social advancement, enriched with instructive historic truths and adorned with the highest strains of poetry before the keel of Cecrops broke the Ægean wave or Cadmus taught his alphabetic mystery to the rude warriors of Thebes.

For the purpose of preparing the Chosen People for their great and distinctive destiny, God established among them peculiar laws and institutions which kept them from mingling with and being contaminated by the demoralizing influences of surrounding nations.

Thus was generated a national pride and *caste* which prevented them from being imitators and copyists, to much extent, of the manners, customs and thoughts of other peoples. After their settlement in Palestine their literature became as distinctive and peculiar as their civil and religious institutions, and for several centuries remained comparatively free from the admixture of foreign elements, and was enlarged and enriched by the productions of native genius. In their national seclusion they studied carefully the rich volume of nature presented in their fertile and beautiful land, and from thence they drew many of their sublime thoughts and appropriate metaphors. With poetic ardor they loved the sweet and quiet vales with murmering streams and gushing springs. To them the odorous breezes were musical as they whispered through olive groves and clustering vineyards, or gently waved the plumed palms; and their souls were filled with emotions of grandeur and sublimity when the fierce storm-king swept the cedar harps of the mountains. Their habits and occupations inclined them to poetic conceptions. Most of them were, in the early periods of their history, husbandmen, vinedressers and shepherds, dwelling in pastoral simplicity in the humble homes for which they had a title from Jehovah. They were not then restless and greedy for gain, but in calm, rural repose, they trusted to the watchful guidance and care of their covenant-keeping God. In this condition of contentment and serenity their minds and hearts were prepared to receive vivid impressions of the beautiful. Day by day they witnessed the soft radiance of the dawn and breathed the fragrance of the morning, and when their pleasant labors were ended they gazed with rapture upon the golden glories of the evening skies. When the early and latter rains came they rejoiced at the prospects of plenty; and at the time of the harvest and the vintage they went forth with gladsome songs to reap the golden sheaves and gather the purple clusters, rich and heavy, for the foaming wine-press. When they drove their bleating flocks to where the pastures were green and the cool waters were flowing, or wandered with their lowing herds upon the breezy hills, their eyes were filled with scenes of quiet beauty, and their minds with glorious thoughts, and these scenes and thoughts were softened and sanctified when the solemn stillness of the night was resting on the slumbering earth.

> When the silvery moonbeams softly glisten
> And all is hushed save the voice of the soul,
> And the silent stars gently wink and listen
> While heaven's eternal melodies roll.

We will not dwell in this place upon the scenery and natural beauties of the land of Palestine, but reserve the subject for consideration in a subsequent lecture.

In our next lecture we will consider the noble language in which Hebrew thought was enshrined and transmitted as a precious and invaluable legacy to all succeeding ages.

LECTURE III.

THE HEBREW AS A POETICAL LANGUAGE.

The poetry of the Hebrews was written in one of the oldest of human languages that has been preserved in a written literature. Some learned philologists were of the opinion that the Hebrew was the original language of man, and was directly communicated to Adam in Paradise, and at the confusion of tongues was preserved by Divine Providence in the family of Heber, who did not engage in the impious work of the tower-builders of Babel. We have the highest authority for believing that there was once an age in which "the whole earth was of one language and of one speech." We also know that God confounded this common language of mankind, and did so for the purpose of scattering them as different peoples over the earth. We have no facts to induce the belief that the original language existed in its primal structure among any of the newly formed races, and there are many plausible conjectures which tend to show the truth of a contrary hypothesis. A common language was a strong bond of union that made the human race one people, and we are inclined to think that when the race was divided into different peoples by the confusion of their speech the original language ceased to have an entire and distinctive existence.

The verbal analogies and affinities which existed in all the primitive languages clearly show that they sprung from the same parent stock, which seems to have perished in furnishing vital sap to its various offshoots.

Much careful investigation has been made, and many plausible theories have been suggested upon this subject, but no conclusion has been reached entirely satisfactory to all learned philologists.

I am of the opinion, from the very limited investigation which I have been able to make, that the Hebrew was a dialect of a language spoken by various ancient Shemitic nations of Western Asia, and was formed into a distinctive language, like other cultivated languages have been formed from grafts without and germs within, and grew with the increasing wants and intelligence of the people.

I am also of the opinion that the antediluvians reached an advanced stage of civilization, which was transmitted by Noah and his family to the post-diluvian races. From this source the Assyrians and Egyptians derived much of that knowledge and culture which enabled them to exhibit such advancement in the arts and sciences at the earliest historic eras. The ancestors of Abraham, although idolaters, were not barbarians, and they possessed an organized language, and perhaps a written literature. This language was carried by Abraham into Canaan, and soon after that period of migration was enlarged and elevated in giving expression to the sublime monotheistic truths and glorious promises which Jehovah communicated to his chosen servant. It also received accessions from the cognate speech of the Canaanitish tribes among whom the Patriarchs dwelt so long in peaceful and familiar intercourse. The descendants of Jacob dwelt for several centuries among the Egyptians, who were the most highly civilized people of that early age, and their superior learning and culture must have had some influence upon the language of the subject race.

The tribes of Isreal cannot properly be considered as a nation until the time of the Exodus, when Moses, by a peculiar code of laws and novel institutions, gave them an independent and distinctive national existence. He was possessed of splendid genius and a strong, practical intellect, and was familiar with all the learning and literary culture of his times; and was, moreover, divinely commissioned and inspired for his great work of liberating his oppressed people, and preparing them to be a peculiar people unto the Lord. For the purpose of effecting this design we may well suppose that he made changes and modifications in the then existing language of his people, so as to suit the conditions of their new and peculiar national life.

I believe that it is now generally agreed among scholars that the art of alphabetic writing existed long anterior to the age of Moses, and that many ancient nations of Asia possessed a written literature. The ancestors of Abraham lived in a land which was the starting point of civilization, and we know that the Hebrew Patriarchs, by their intelligence and force of character, occupied a distinguished position among their Canaanitish and Phœnician neighbors. We may well suppose that the chosen people, with their many advantages, were not destitute of the learning and arts which existed in their age in the country in which they sojourned, and in the immediate vicinity. For more than a century after their migration into Egypt they were in much favor with the kings and nobility of that highly civilized people. They must have had at least some memorials consisting of well defined traditions of ancestral history, earnest hymns of thanksgiving and praise; and many important events must have been commemorated by ballads and songs, the voices of their intelligent thought-life and elevated affections and emotions. It requires no unreasonable stretch of fancy to suppose that such a people had made as great advancement as other nations with whom they were in constant association. Some scholars think that the book of Genesis contains portions of various smaller books which were the sacred literature of the Patriarchal Church, and were in the possession of the Hebrews while in Egypt, and were combined and enlarged by Moses under the guidance of the Holy Spirit. Upon this subject there is much contrariety of opinion among Biblical scholars, and I have not the space in a lecture, or the learning properly to discuss the matter.

We believe that the Pentateuch in its present literary form is the work of Moses. We think we are sustained in this opinion by the internal evidence which the work affords, and by the uniform history and traditions of the Hebrew nation. We find the Pentateuch in a language of mature development in the earliest periods of Hebrew national history, and it was always regarded with sacred veneration by the nation, and as the standard of their literary culture.

Some philologists suppose that Moses was the author of the written language of the Hebrews and formed it as a sacred language under the same divine influence which inspired him with supernatural wisdom in constructing his civil and religious institutions. In studying God's wondrous plan in developing human civilization, there is no necessity for supposing the exertion of His miraculous power, where results can be reasonably accounted for by natural causes and processes controlled by His usual providences. Be this as it may, the fact that such a sublime literature and language existed among the Hebrews at such an early period of their national existence furnishes strong evidence that they were an intellectual people of considerable culture. They had been much demoralized by the oppressions of a hard bondage and by the corrupting influences of Egyptian society, and this literature was intended to produce a moral regeneration, and before the end of the long desert pilgrimage this object was, in some degree, accomplished. They frequently heard the reading of their history and laws; they witnessed the grand and awful manifestations at Sinai; the imposing services of the Tabernacle; the numerous beneficences of Jehovah, and His just and severe chastisements. This discipline of the desert, and the wise instructions, the patient forbearance and paternal care of Moses greatly elevated the character of the Hebrews and prepared them for their noble destiny in the Promised Land.

As we cannot read the Hebrew language, in speaking of its force, richness and beauty we can only express some of the opinions of scholars who have written upon the subject. This language is peculiar for the number of verbs and their derivatives that abound in its structure. In every language the verb is the animating power, the vital principle, that gives the force, energy and beauty of human thought and emotion. Herder says, "in the Hebrew the verb is almost the whole of the language. It is an abyss of verbs, a sea of billows, where motion, action rolls on without end." He makes the language speak and say, "I live, move and act. Tne senses and the passions, not abstract reasoners and philosophers, were my creators. Thus I am formed for poetry, nay, my whole essence is poetry." That eloquent poet and learned and accomplished Hebraist also remarks that the language is barren of mere abstract terms, but rich in words representing sentiment, passion, emotion and the various objects of nature. "It is the very breath of the soul. It does not claim the beauty of sound like the Greek, but it breathes and lives. Such it is to us who are but partially acquainted with its pronunciation, and for whom its deeper gutturals remain unuttered and unutterable. In those old times when the soul was unshackled, what fullness of emotion, what store of words that breathe must have inspired it. It was, to use an expression of its own," "The spirit of God that spake in it. The breath of the Almighty that gave it life." Such was the language in which the thoughts, feelings and emotions of the ancient Hebrews were enshrined and transmitted to succeeding ages. We have but little information as to the growth of the Hebrew language during the commonwealth which existed for four hundred years. The books of Joshua, Judges and Ruth contain a short and fragmentary history of those times, but they were probably written in a subsequent age. We know, however, from the writings which certainly existed before and after the commonwealth that no marked dialectical or idiomatic changes were made in the vocabulary or structure of the *cultured* and *literary* language.

The Pentateuch possessed such inherent literary excellence, was so full of the highest wisdom, was so frequently read and studied and was so devoutly venerated by the people, that in the midst of so many national vicisitudes it preserved the literary language from any change but that of very gradual development. Although we have so few literary remains of those times we are well satisfied that the people did not live in a condition of intellectual sloth and barrenness. They often violated their covenant with Jehovah and were visited with the severe chastisements of His corrective providence, but they enjoyed long intervals of prosperity, peace and divine favor, and observed the laws and institutions established by Moses for the promotion of intellectual and moral culture. Toward the close of the commonwealth the Hebrews had reached such a condition of intelligence as to require a more enlightened system of mental and religious instruction than that afforded by the Priests and Levites, and to meet this requirement Samuel organized the Schools of the Prophets. Up to that time the Pentateuch was the library of their legal and religious literature and the chief repository of the vocabulary of their sacred and cultivated language, but the active and inventive intellect, and the highly imaginative and emotional nature of the people must have produced a rich and varied literature, the outgrowth of their social and domestic condition, and expressed in the popular dialect of common life. That was the poetical and heroic age, and from the few glimpses which we have of its history we feel sure that it was full of scenes and events well calculated to arouse the emotions and inspire the genius of an earnest and imaginative race, and like other primitive peoples, they must have expressed their vivid conceptions and fervid emotions in the language of poetry and song. The Hebrews of subsequent times regarded the period of the commonwealth as a glorious era in their history, and with patriotic affection and pride they cherished the ballads, songs and traditions of their heroic ancestry.

The Hebrew language reached its highest condition of culture in the age of David and Solomon, and from the time of Hezekiah it commenced to decline by the commixture of foreign elements, and almost ceased to be a spoken language during the Babylonish captivity. The Hebrews were in captivity only seventy years, and yet when a small portion of two of the tribes, called from about that time Jews, returned from exile, there were only a few of the most learned scribes who could write, translate or speak the noble language of their forefathers.

The Jews never spoke or became familiar with the old language, and the Scriptures used in the synagogue worship were translated by interpreters into the Aramaic tongue until the Septuagint version furnished the Scriptures in a rich and beautiful language, understood by all intelligent Jews who dwelt in the limits of the Alexandrian Empire. Among the educated Jews who dwelt in Palestine and Babylon the old Hebrew still remained as the language of literature and as it was used by the Rabbins and learned Doctors of the Law. The Hebrew never again became a vernacular speech. Portions of the Latin and Greek still exist as living elements in some of the languages of Modern Europe, but the old Hebrew as a vital speech no longer breathes from living lips, and its thoughts are alone embalmed in the hearts and memories of mankind.

Although we cannot fully comprehend the accents and cadences of dead languages, they are well adapted for the preservation of the thoughts and characteristics of nations. They are stereotyped in form and are not subject to the changes and modifications of a living speech. They retain much of the force and brilliancy of national thought, but as they lose the rhythm, harmony and passionate energy of pronunciation they do not fully represent the fervid emotions and affections that animated the hearts of the people.

Although so many historic truths and literary treasures are embalmed in a dead language, still it is like a gallery of painting and statuary. In the productions of the painter we see and admire skillful imitation and delicacy of finish, but we know that the copied scenes and objects do not equal the living and glowing beauties of nature which inspired the genius of the artist.

The most perfect statue, wrought with exquisite and marvelous skill, and combining the beauties and excellences selected from various living forms by the quick discerning eye and cultivated taste of the artist, are inadequate representations of the animated forms of symmetry and grace, which inspire the heart with purer and nobler emotions of the beautiful than the highest ideals of genius.

Apelles, with matchless skill, painted Campaspe and won the favor and gold of Alexander, but he could not copy that inimitable beauty which inspired his heart with a love dearer to him than wealth and immortal fame.

All the voices of the past are voices from the grave. Nations, although dead, still speak through their preserved literatures and teach us much valuable knowledge, but we cannot hear the glowing and thrilling eloquence and tender pathos of the living speech that once so intensely expressed their varied thoughts and emotions.

In the natural world we can find many illustrations of the familiar truth which we have presented, but we will make only one reference. A frozen stream may be as clear as crystal and sparkle and gleam in the sunlight, but it has none of the motion and melody of the living waters as they murmur among the rocks or ripple on the sandy shore. In one condition the stream is invested and surrounded by the brilliant but cold beauties of nature, while in the other it flows onward in musical tones amid the bloom, verdure and freshness of Spring and the golden richness of the Summer.

The old Hebrew language has uttered no living voice for more than twenty centuries, and the most learned Hebraist of our times, after the deep silence of so many ages, cannot revive the cadences of its pronunciation, and thus form an adequate conception of the liquid flow and melody of those grand anthems, that, on the waves of music and song, swelled through the courts and porches of Solomon's "magnifical temple;" or feel the full force of those sublime and eloquent rhapsodies which Isaiah, with fervid heart and burning lip, once uttered to his rebellious and disobedient countrymen.

We judge of the variety, extent and wealth of a nation's thought from the copiousness of language preserved in its literature. Language is a symbol of ideas, and is gradually formed and extended by the operation of the national mind. It is the embodiment of national thought, and enables us to feel, in some degree, the pulse throbs of the national heart. In the refined and cultivated language of a people we find their most elevated and matured thoughts, but their elegant literature does not contain much of the simple dialects which vividly expressed the earnest feelings and sentiments of the common people in private life, and which often glowed with exquisite gems of poetry.

Who can ever forget or undervalue the treasures which Burns has contributed to our literature by his matchless songs and poems written in the Doric dialect of humble life, full of vivid pictures, and expressing, in such simple and tender pathos, the feelings and sentiments of his peasant countrymen. In his simple home songs beautiful thoughts and fancies sparkle and gleam around his rhythmic words like sunshine and dew drops upon the fresh flowers of the morning.

The books of the Old Testament contain the remains of Hebrew literature produced during the period when the language was spoken. These books were written under divine inspiration and were intended principally for the specific purpose of developing the riligious life of the Chosen People. They furnish many domestic and social scenes of exquisite beauty, but they, by no means, contain the entire literature of the home life of the Hebrews. Nearly all of this literature has been lost, and with it much of the variety and richness of the language, thought and emotions of the nation.

From the various translations of the Old Testament the learned philologist is enabled to make a comparative estimate of the richness and variety of the vocabulary of the original tongue. This experiment has been made by accomplished scholars, and they have found that in words expressing passionate energy, affection and the fervent emotions of the soul, and in giving distinctive descriptions of the various objects of nature the Hebrew has a more copious and appropriate vocabulary than the Greek, the Latin or the English. Such classes of words in every language are principally used by poets, and from these comparative estimates we may readily conclude that the Hebrews were endowed with higher poetic capacities and sensibilities than those refined and richly gifted nations whose immortal works of genius constitute the great mass of classical literature.

Every literary production is deprived of much of its original power and beauty by translation, although it may be translated into a language of more extensive verbal resources and higher culture. A little flower taken from an Alpine cliff and transplanted into a warm and fertile garden in the valley loses the delicate tints of coloring which adorned it while blooming amid eternal frosts on the verge of the avalanche.

Every literary production was the outgrowth of popular taste and feeling, and exhibited its purest beauty and exerted its greatest influence among the people for whom it was originally intended.

Translations of the rude ballads and war songs of the Scandinavian Scalds produce in us none of the enthusiasm and lofty courage with which they inspired the hearts of the old Vikings and their followers as they fought in bloody forays, or struggled with the cold storms and waves of the northern seas.

Pope, one of the most gifted and accomplished of English poets, spent many years in the laborious and careful translation of the Iliad. He gave a classic to literature which glitters with the wealth and rhythmic elegance of the English language, but it is wanting in that mystic power of genius with which the Blind Harper electrified the proud cities of Hellas and Ionia, and threw the halo of immortal fame around the valiant heroes who fought before the walls of Troy.

An American audience of the highest classic culture would not listen with any degree of patience to the repetition in our language, by the most gifted and accomplished histrionic artist, of those tragedies which once made the statesmen, warriors, philosophers, orators and poets of Athens weep for the misfortunes of the ill-fated Œdipus and the heroic Antigone, and listen with breathless awe to the story of the wronged, forsaken and revengeful Medea.

Who can now feel the full force of that eloquence which once rang with sublime thoughts and rich cadences over the temple-crowned Acropolis, and which Phillip of Macedon dreaded more than all the armies of Greece?

Who can now comprehend the magic power of that magnificent oratory by which the timid Tully controlled the destinies of war-loving Rome?

No translator can do full justice to the literature of an ancient and dead language, as he is incapable of catching the spirit and inherent beauties of the original. There are idiomatic peculiarities about the old Hebrew which present many difficulties to translators in obtaining the true spirit and rhythm of the original. It is very ancient, and there is no cognate contemporary literature with which it can be be compared, and which might aid in elucidating linguistic obscurities. The writers of the Old Testament were under the guidance of the Holy Spirit and translators cannot feel the divine afflatus which inspired the hearts and genius of the old Hebrew prophets and bards.

The Hebrew letters in present use date no further back than to the time of the captivity, and the vowel points and accents used in the connection of syllables, words and sentences, serve but to show how the Jewish scholars of subsequent times expressed the Hebrew when these changes were introduced, and how they themselves understood the text. The ancient Hebrew, in which the Old Testament was originally written, was a pure consonantal text, and the consonants were so arranged as to indicate the appropriate vowel sounds to a reader familiar with the living language. The vowels were unseen, and circulated as the blood of the language. But after the old Hebrew lost the force and freedom of a living tongue these phonetic and fluent elements of speech could not be fully understood and properly applied so as to bring out its entire richness and melody. The sublimity of thought, the historical value and the credibility of the Old Testament still remained—it lost only its original literary form to some extent. The notation of vowels and accents, made after the language ceased to be spoken, supplied, in some degree, its flexibility and elasticity, and made it utter many of its ancient voices of emotion and melody which thrill the souls of mankind.

The Old Testament has been remarkably well translated into the English language. More than half of the words of our English version are Anglo-Saxon, a language eminent for its simplicity, terseness and power of expression—some of the characteristics of the old Hebrew. The English Bible is the grandest and most beautiful book in our literature. It owes some of its literary excellence and form to the rich, forcible and rhythmic flow of the English tongue, but the grand thoughts and graphic pictures that illumine its pages are the products of the Hebrew mind, which have lost much of their force and exquisite literary excellence and beauty in passing into translation. The sunlight in passing through the *camera* depicts with accuracy and beauty the human face and the grand objects of nature, but the sketching sunbeams do not fasten the glow that beams around the objects which are copied. Thus our English Bible furnishes but a photographic picture of Hebrew life, and does not give the full literary force and beauty of the thoughts and eloquent utterances of the old Hebrew bards which awakened such thrilling emotions in the hearts of old Israel.

All philologist agree that the etymology and structure of a language, its peculiar idioms and dialects, and the changes which it undergoes in the process of development, furnish important information as to the characteristics of a people. Language is the voice of the thought and emotional life of a nation, and is necessarily a valuable portion of its history. The old Hebrew, although imperfectly understood, furnishes internal evidence that it was formed and spoken by a noble people of high mental and moral culture who lived in primeval times, in pastoral simplicity and in a beautiful land and clime. It is emphatically a religious and emotional language, formed, from infancy to mature development, as it were, in the presence of Jehovah and by His immediate tuition, and influenced by grand events and wondrous providences.

The Aramaic, spoken by the Jews after their return from the exile in Babylon, plainly shows the intellectual and moral degeneracy produced by captivity, calamity and servitude. They had forgotten the noble language of their fathers and spoke in the rugged tongue of their heathen conquerors, and yet this language of slavery was glorified by the utterance of divine truths. It was the original language of the Sermon on the Mount and the beautiful and inimitable parables of our Saviour.

The Greek, so soft, so sweet, so expressive, so rich in classic elegance and so harmonious in cadences, enables us to form an incomplete but still vivid conception of the acute, subtle, enlightened and imaginative race who lived in the refined age when Pericles ruled, when Callistratus reared and Phidias adorned the Parthenon.

The sonorous and stately rhythm of the Latin shows that it was the language of a brave, aggressive and imperial people, and it sounds like the martial music that regulated the measured tread of those invincible legions who carried their victorious eagles into every land.

The Italian is the voice of that civilization which reared the splendid basilicas and gorgeous palaces of Catholic Rome, woke into melody the strings of Dante's and Petrarch's lyre, and guided the pencil and chisel of Raphael and Angelo as they formed those ideal creations which have been the matchless models of art.

In the Spanish we can distinctly trace the commingled elements of Roman civilization and Gothic vigor, tinged with the Oriental culture of the Caliphs. The peculiar features of the language, and the stern, bigoted and relentless character of the Spaniard, were both formed in that long, fierce and bloody conflict of eight hundred years between the Moore and the Goth—the Crescent and the Cross.

The French is as soft, as gay and as versatile as the brilliant women and accomplished courtiers who once bowed the knee to royalty in the gilded saloons of Versailles; and it is filled with the accents of the rich and melodious speech of sunny Provence in which the Troubadours sang the songs of love, chivalry and old romance.

The German is the remarkable language of a remarkable people. It has a rich and extensive vocabulary derived almost entirely from an original stock, and has less commixture of foreign elements than any other language of Europe. It has a wonderful capability of developing itself from its own substance. It seems to grow and expand like a giant oak that has been strengthened by the sunshine and storms of centuries, deriving its sap from its ancient roots, and ever extending its branches covered with fresh, rich and living verdure and beauty. The Germans have preserved more than any other nation of Modern Europe the distinguishing characteristics of their remote ancestors. Although their country has so long been the battlefield of contending nations, they are still the truest representatives of the Teuton race. Their national progress seems to have been the result of inherent resources called into active and energizing life by the Reformation, and their language was solidified and enriched by Luther's version of the Bible. They have wrought out for themselves a grand and distinctive literature and now occupy one of the highest intellectual thrones among mankind.

In the English we find the language of a free, progressive, world-impressing and world-embracing people. It has drawn treasures from nearly every literature and continues to expand in richness and fullness as the enlightened mind achieves new conquests in the various realms of human thought. In the vocabulary of this language we can distinctly trace its origin back to that remarkable people, who, from the disintegrating elements of ancient civilization, created the nations and the civil institutions of Modern Europe; and we can also readily distinguish the proportions and relations of the various races that were combined in the formation of the English people. The principle elements of the English language are derived from the Anglo Saxon and the Latin, the noble languages in which are enshrined the principles of freedom, justice and enlightened jurisprudence, and the highest intellectual achievements of mankind.

If we had not reached the reasonable limits of this lecture we would be pleased to consider more fully than we have heretofore done the wonderful and controlling influences which the Hebrew Scriptures through various versions have exerted upon the languages, literatures and civilizations of all subsequent ages. We feel that it would be improper for us, in a brief and cursory manner to speak upon such a rich, important and extensive theme.

God divided mankind into various races by the confusion of tongues at Babel, but His revealed word for centuries has been exerting a reverse influence in bringing different nations into closer connection and fellowship by establishing a common literature which is ever tending to a unification of all of the children of men. The invention of printing has, under divine providence, enabled the Christian Church to multiply copies of the Bible by millions and in nearly all the languages of mankind. It now has the Pentecostal gift of the Holy Spirit and all the nations hear it speak to them in their own tongues the wonderful works of God.

Withou entering into an extended argument to sustain our conclusion, we venture to express the belief that the English speaking peoples, with their enlightened laws and institutions of freedom; with their incomparable literature and with their rich, extensive, diversified and rapidly expanding language, all moulded and invigorated by the Bible, are destined in the providence of God to be the leading actors in evangelizing and civilizing the world, and binding the various races of men in the bonds of Christian brotherhood.

LECTURE IV.

The Style of Hebrew Poetry.

In judging of the beauties and excellencies of the style of Hebrew poetry we can gain but little assistance from the principles and rules of poetic art and criticism which have been established in other nations. It is so essentially different from all other poetry in its structure that we can hardly institute any comparison.

The Greeks sought to regulate all of their fine arts by beauty and harmony of proportions and relations, and were as carefully artistic in their metrical arrangement of poetry as in the production of their elegant statuary and architecture. In their poetry we find the exquisite productions of linguistic and metrical art which have exerted a refining influence upon the poetry of subsequent ages.

The use of rhyme in modern poetry has contributed to its harmony of diction, but fettered the bold, strong and sublime energies of creative genius. The origin of rhyme is involved in obscurity, but it certainly did not exist to much extent in the poetry of the Hebrews and of the classic productions of antiquity. Rhyme is a creation of modern art, while rhythm springs from the love which exists in the human soul for order, harmony and beauty, and spontaneously gushes out in music and song. Rhythm of language has existed in all ages, and among most of the civilized nations has been regulated by certain well defined technical rules which constitute the art of poetry.

Hebrew poetry in the original language must have been full of rhythm, as this characteristic is not lost by translation into the rudest and most inharmonious speech. This rhythm existed both in words and thoughts, and is so inherent and vital that the more literal any translation of Hebrew poetry the greater are the beauties and melodies which it transfuses into the foreign tongue. This peculiarity does not exist to the same extent in any other literature. Literal translations of ancient classic poetry into our language are always prosaic, and the affluent versatility of genius is required to give them the rhythm and spirit of poetry.

The rhythm and poetry of the Old Testament Scriptures are not confined to the strictly poetical books, but sentences and verses of the finest poetry are found interspersed in rich profusion in all their legal and historical books. These poetic sentences and verses gleam like jewels encased in gold, and the prevalence of such an element in their didactic writings furnishes high evidence of the imaginative temperament and genius of the Hebrew people.

Although Hebrew poetry is so full of rhythm and melody there is much doubt as to whether it was originally regulated by any fixed and invariable rules of metrical structure. This subject has called forth much ingenius discussion and elaborate investigation, and still no definite conclusions have been made which are entirely satisfactory to Biblical critics and scholars. The pronunciation of the language and its laws of syllabic quantity and accentuation have long been lost, and the rules of its metrical arrangement can never be correctly ascertained, as mankind can never again hear its living tones.

Some writers have contended that the existence of such rules of metrical arrangement can reasonably be inferred from well established facts in Hebrew history. Music and poetry are twin sisters of art and exert an influence upon each other. The sacred writings frequently mention various kinds of musical instruments, and music and poetry were the subjects of study in the Schools of the Prophets. The Hebrews celebrated their domestic and social festivals, their victories and parts of their religious services with songs, instrumental music and the sacred dance. From these well attested historical facts the argument has been made that a people so familiar with the melodies of sound and the graceful harmony of motion could not have failed to perceive and appreciate the pleasing rhythm and melody produced in language by the proper adjustment of words and sentences, and that this natural perception would necessarily have soon suggested and formed artificial rules of metrical structure.

As we have no knowledge of the etymology and grammatical structure of the Hebrew language we are not qualified to express an opinion upon any internal evidence which it furnishes as to the artificial metrical arrangement of the Hebrew poetry. As translated in our English Bible we find that the Psalms need none of the rules of classic and modern versification to bring out their melody, beauty of imagery and sublimity of thought, and when chanted in the Church service they blend in sweet unison with the splendid harmonies of the organ. We know of no reason why Hebrew poetry should not have possessed the same natural capabilities in the original language when chanted in accompaniment to the instruments of music in the Temple service.

When the Psalms were introduced into the liturgical services of the Temple they must have been so arranged and adapted to accompanying instruments of music as to be sung in unison by the Levitical choirs and the congregation, but we are inclined to think that no fixed rules of art controlled the authors in their original composition.

The Hebrew Bards were men of intense thoughts, emotions and purposes, and their minds and hearts were occupied in contemplating the grandest subjects. Their poems were not simply the products of the imagination, but were full of the solemn realities of eventful history and their own personal experiences and emotions; their joys, their sorrows, their faith, their love for God and their devout ascriptions of thanksgiving and praise.

They were poets born, not made, and the breathings of the Holy Spirit inspired their minds and animated their hearts, and they uttered great truths, not only for their own times, but for all the coming ages; and their earnest thoughts and intense emotions were expressed in appropriate words, which were naturally arranged into rhythmic cadences. They were under the guidance of that Omniscience and Omnipotence which has filled the natural world in infinite variety with a melody, beauty and sublimity far surpassing the productions of the most exalted human genius.. What were the hanging gardens of Babylon and the sumptuous palaces of Assyria, the massive pyramids and grand temples of Egypt when compared with the excellency of Carmel, the glory of Lebanon and the grandeur of Hermon crowned with eternal snow and yet robed in garments of verdure bright with flowers and sparkling with dews? What are all the parks and gardens which human art has so elaborately arranged and beautified to gratify the pride and cultivated taste of the proud and great when compared with the majestic primeval forest intersected with noble rivers gleaming in sunshine or sparkling with the light of stars, and the wild gardens which God has planted on the fertile hillsides and in luxuriant valleys filled with exhuberant fruitfulness and picturesque loveliness.

Nature needs none of the aids of human skill to regulate her voices of melody. The birds know no rules of art as they sing their joyous lyrics. The winds and storms—those wild, mighty and mysterious singers—observe no certain metre when they hold their concerts among the woodlands and the hills. No mortal corypheus leads the choir of the jubilant rills, bounding cataracts and solemn flowing rivers as they rehearse their eternal hymns, and God alone touches the organ keys of the ocean and makes the billows swell in glorious symphonies over the vasty deep and sound in sobbing tones or sublime anthems on every shore. The finite mind of man may not be able to comprehend and his heart to feel the divine harmonies of the vast orchestra of nature, but in the ear of the Infinite Leader of the choir of the universe they are ever rehearsing aright a grand oratorio.

With the exception of a few alphabetic and alliterative poems found in the Old Testament Scriptures, the traces of artificial metrical arrangement in Hebrew poetry are too variant and indistinct to form any definite and coherent system of poetic art.

The Hebrew bards fully understood the energy and power of their language and also its capability of cadence and harmony, and the sublime truths and thoughts given and controlled by divine inspiration were expressed in vivid and appropriate words and imagery, attended with a thrilling rhythm of utterance which was natural and not artificial. They were profoundly conscious of the diverse emotions of the human soul and of the grandeur and varied beauties of nature, but they never indulged in glowing sentimentalism and extended picturesque description, which have employed so much of the elegant diction of classic and modern poetic art. Their symbols and metaphors were not used as graceful figures of rhetoric, but as illustrations of divine attributes and to enforce the great truths that absorbed all their thoughts. Their enthusiasm was too intense and their conceptions too vivid to be trammelled by any rigid rules of art. They were nature's poets and God's messengers to mankind, and their messages were for all the ages and were expressed in language to touch the chords of every human heart.

We will now consider briefly the most plausible system of rules which have been presented as to the artificial structure of Hebrew poetry. Since the delivery of the justly celebrated lectures of Bishop Lowth, the various styles of Hebrew poetry have generally been included under the generic name of parallelism. It is insisted that such a poetic structure is not found to much extent in any other literature. He defines the term to mean a certain correspondence in words, sentences and thoughts in parallel lines. Subsequent critics and scholars have suggested additions and modifications to Bishop Lowth's system, and presented many illustrative examples, but all concede that there is an obvious rhythmical symmetry of words, thoughts and members. This symmetry in Hebrew poetry has been very appropriately styled "thought rhythm," as all the ideas conveyed are in harmonious accord, and in unison with the finest and purest affections, sentiments and feelings of man's moral and religious nature. It does not need the elaborate elegance and delicate finish of art to display its excellence, but with simple and inherent power it wakens a melody in the soul which words cannot fully express, but which is breathed in longing aspirations for a higher, holier and immortal life. The parallelistic arrangement certainly exists in the structure of Hebrew poetry. It may not be as pleasing to an artistic and cultivated taste as the euphony of rhyme or the modulated metre and musical flow of blank verse and the classic hexameter, but its comparatively inartificial structure allowed greater freedom in the use of words and sentences, and was thus better suited to express the grand and lofty conceptions and emotions of an earnest, impassioned, imaginative and primitive people.

We have a very limited knowledge upon this subject, but it seems to us that too great a variety of species of parallelism have been presented to admit of any definite laws regulating their artificial structure.

Bishop Lowth divides the parallelism into three distinctive species, to which we will briefly refer, without giving his full definitions and illustrations.

The *synonymous* parallelism is more frequently used than any other, and consists in the repetition of the same sentiment in parallel lines in different but equivalent terms. In illustrating this species of parallelism, an English poet and critic finely remarked, "In repeating the same idea in different words the Hebrew muse seems as if displaying a fine opal that discovers fresh beauty in every new light in which it is turned. Numerous and beautiful passages in the Old Testament might be cited as examples of this kind of parallelism.

The *antithetic* parallelism was also used by the Hebrew bards in their didactic and sententious poetry when anything was illustrated by its contrary being placed in opposition, thus,

> The heaven is my throne and
> The earth is my footstool,

showing the importance and grandeur of one over the other. And again, as setting forth the greatness, majesty and glory of God, as compared with man.

> It is He that sitteth upon the circle of the earth,
> And the inhabitants thereof are as grasshoppers.

I am not able to form a clear and satisfactory conception of the *synthetic* parallelism from the definition of Bishop Lowth. He says, in substance, that it consists only in the similar form of construction of sentences in which there is some correspondence and equality between different propositions. He also says: "The degrees of the correspondence of the lines of this sort of parallels must, from the nature of it, be various. Sometimes the parallelism is more, sometimes less exact, sometimes hardly apparent."

While there is some general resemblance between many of the illustrative examples given by writers on this subject, yet in nearly every instance there is some marked diversity. Most of such examples are highly poetic in sentiment and diction, and may be classed together on account of their general similitude, but they manifest no artistic intention of making them similar in literary structure. They may be compared to the mountains which God has constructed. Between the separate elevations of a mountain range there is a correspondence in form and nature, as they are all mountains rising from the valleys toward the heavens, and yet they all have many distinctive features, and together they form a grand and imposing prospect as they gleam with the beauty of the sunlight, or are dimly discovered through their misty veils, or are seen robed with the tranquil azure of the distance. Thus the elevated thoughts and feelings of the inspired bards were constructed into resembling forms of poetic language, rhythmical in cadences and glowing with truth and beauty, without any artistic intention in the choice of words and the structure of sentences. We often find the various species of parallelism so closely and intimately intermingled that they cannot be separated without disturbing the harmony and beauty of the composition.

In Isaiah's description of the coming golden age of the Messiah, we find, not only the three species of parallelism designated by Bishop Lowth, but many other forms of Hebrew poetry. They were combined and blended into a magnificent synthetic poem, not by any rules of poetic art, but by the untrammelled power of divine inspiration and the highest genius. It is a splendid outburst of poetic rapture, produced by the glorious scenes of the coming future that gleamed with celestial radiance upon the spiritual vision of the prophet bard. The language in which he pictured his vivid imagery, and expressed his sublime thoughts, gushed from his mind and heart in spontaneous freedom, purity, beauty and liquid melody, just like the crystal, musical and leaping rills flow from the sides of Hermon to form the rolling and swelling Jordan.

I will not refer to the other species of parallelism pointed out by learned Biblical critics and scholars. The diversity of species and examples which they present tend to show that the Hebrew bards were not controlled by fixed rules of art in the structure of the parallelism. The Hebrew parallelism, consisting of brief, sententious and simple propositions in parallel lines, was a natural and not an artificial arrangement of language, and was not metrical in its structure. Exactness, uniformity, regularity, skill, and strict carefulness are some of the properties and rules of art in the construction of poetic composition. The productions of the Hebrew bards seem to be the spontaneous outgushing of fervid thoughts and feelings glowing with imagery and rhythmical with natural melodies.

Nature seems to use the principle of the parallelism of resemblance, comparison or contrast in displaying many of her highest beauties and sublimest objects, but uses it in infinite variety, as did the Hebrew bards. The ocean rolling billow after billow on the shore and yet each billow having a slightly variant sound, produced by the diverse influences of the changeful winds and the ebbing and flowing tides, is a striking example of nature's synonymous parallelism. We often see an antithetic parallelism in nature when a dark and stormy night is followed by a clear morning, and the tranquil skies are beautifully blue, and soft melodies are floating on the balmy air, and the sportive sunbeams are sparkling and glowing on the rich and dewy verdure of the landscape.

The still vast night when the stars in serene and silvery brightness are moving through the dark fields of immensity in ceaseless and glorious march around a grand central and controlling orb in the far distant regions of the universe, is a synthetic poem of wondrous beauty and impressive grandeur.

The beauty and expressiveness of symbols, metaphors,

parables and allegories are in a great degree dependent upon the parallelism which they present. How often do we see in poetry and prose a parallelism between the seasons of the year and the different periods of human life. The Spring is youth with its brightness, freshness and hope; the Summer is manhood with its ardor, passionate energy and development of power; Autumn is the time of fruition, repose and gentle decline, and hoary Winter is the season of old age, decrepitude and death. The whole realm of nature and the departments of art are full of rich, varied and beautiful parallelisms which are sources of poetic inspiration and intellectual pleasures.

We will not dwell longer upon the subject of parallelisms which are generally conceded to be characteristic peculairities of Hebrew poetry. We will not further consider the vexed question, whether Hebrew poetry in connection with the parallelism had any artificial rules of metrical arrangement. A knowledge of the rules of Hebrew metre, if any ever existed, might satisfy the eager curiosity of archæologists but would not contribute much to the enlightenment of mankind. The spirit of Hebrew poetry is immortal and its beauty of imagery and sublimity, its tearful pathos and its holy and blessed truths are transfused into every language in which the Bible has been translated.

The style of the Hebrew bards is highly symbolic and metaphorical. Many of the symbols and metaphors were derived from familiar natural objects and the scenes and occurances of social and domestic life, which gave simplicity to their poetry and made it more pleasing and intelligible to the popular mind. How frequent and how beautiful are the illustrations which they derived from the animal and vegetable kingdoms and from the broad fields of the earth and the skies. The rose, the lily, the vine, the figtree, the cedar and palm, and other trees and flowers, are interwoven in their garlands of song, fresh in living verdure, fragrant with rich perfumes and sparkling with dews. In referring to the rich fancy of the Hebrew poets in the natural world we may liken them to the Psalmists' discription of the dove, whose wings are " covered with silver and her feathers with yellow gold;" and they often mounted on wings as eagles and soared to the home of the thunder and storm and to the still higher regions of immensity and unclouded light; and on the wings of the morning they went to the uttermost parts of the sea, and everywhere found the majesty, the power, the goodness and the glory of God.

The Hebrew poets also invested inanimate objects with the attributes of sentient life. To them the harmonious voices of the hills, woods and streams; the deep tones of the thunder, the tempest and restless sea were intelligible utterances and were translated into their poetry. To them the roar of the lion, the screams of the eagle, the songs of the birds and the chirps of insects were filled with poetic meaning. The description of the warhorse in Job is intensely poetical. It is more picturesque and glowing than a painting. The pen of inspired genius is far more graphic than the pencil of art.

The Hebrew poets felt that they lived in a grand sanctified earthly temple, luminous with the presence of Jehovah, decorated with the beauties of nature which He had formed, and ever sounding with multitudinous tones of melody. Every object and living creature that surrounded them were animated with an intelligent and communing spirit, ever teaching the love and watchful care of an invisible but omnipotent Father. The Hebrew bards truly " looked through nature up to nature's God" and from him and the works of His hands received their sublime inspiration. They loved to hear the voices of nature and see her various beauties; and she taught them to modulate their melodies of language, and furnished their glorious imagery. They were also familiar with the harmonies of the human heart when swelling with enthusiasm, bounding with joy, sobbing with sorrow or breathing out the earnest and reverential accents of thanksgiving and praise.

Much of the Hebrew poetry was lyrical, and, even in our language, has a pleasing rhythmic flow which is easily adapted to elegant music. The book of Psalms, called in the Hebrew language "The Book of Praises," is a collection of sacred lyrics. The name given this book in the Septuagint version clearly shows that the Psalms were chanted in accompaniment to stringed instruments of music. The Word Psalm was derived from a Greek verb signifying "to touch or strike a chord.".

We have abundant evidence for believing that the Hebrews were fond of music and attained high excellence in that beautiful art. From various examples recorded in the Old Testament, and from the form of most of their lyrical productions we may properly conclude that their sacred hymns were from the earliest times chanted in responsive melodies. This was the manner prescribed by David for the Temple service, and the Priests and Levites responded in alternate choirs. Isaiah describes the Seraphim as chanting in the same manner the praises of Jehovah in the Heavenly Temple

> "Holy! Holy! Holy! is the Lord of Hosts
> The whole earth is full of His glory."

The antiphonal or responsive style of chanting sacred hymns was used by the Greeks and other ancient nations and was almost invariably adopted in the Christian Churhes of the patristic ages.

Neither the Hebrews, the Greeks or any other nation of antiquity had a full knowledge of the delicacy, variety and richness of the harmony of sounds which have added so much to the glory of music in modern times. Among the ancients music was simply an art, now it may be regarded as an elegant and complicated science. This advancement of music had its origin at an early age in the religious services of the Christian Church. Christian music exerted a refining and elevating influence, and together with Christian art and poetry greatly assisted in producing the splendid æsthetic culture of modern civilization. Music as a science combines melody and harmony. The technical signification of melody is an arrangement in succession of different sounds of the same voice or instrument. Harmony is the result of the union of two or more concording musical sounds. When properly attuned musical strings of varying tones are struck in pleasing succession melody is produced. When two or more strings that are in unison are touched at the same time their sounds blend into harmony. There may be melody without harmony, but harmony is always the union of melodies. The varying notes of the bird, the diverse whisperings of the breezes and the continuous murmurings of the rills are full of melody, but such sounds are not in artistic harmony.

The musical instruments of the ancient nations were rude and simple and not capable of much delicacy, variety and compass of accordant sounds. The skillful performer could produce the mazy running melodies of sound but could not waken many accordant notes and combine and blend them in sweet harmonies. We know, however that ancient music had an enlivening, stirring and even enrapturing effect upon the hearers. How often in Grecian history and literature do we read of the magical influence of the Doric flute and the Lesbian lyre. The timbrels of Miriam and her maidens accompanying the chorus of the triumphal hymn of Moses, filled the hearts of rescued Israel with holy raptures; and the witchery of David's harp exorcised the evil spirit from the bosom of Saul.

The effects of music depend in a great degree upon attendant circumstances and the feelings and tastes of the hearers. The sublime oratorios of Handel, Mozart and

Beethoven are universally admired by the Christian world, as they awaken in every mind and heart grand associations of thought and holy emotions.

The elegant and complex opera may be highly appreciated by cultivated musical amateurs whose ears are attuned to delicate, various and nicely blending harmonies, but we find that the sweet melodies of the simple songs that are sung in *solo* always produce the *encoring* outburst of popular appreciation and applause. The wild Indian would listen with stolid indifference to the sublimest and most finished production of musical genius, when a rude war-song of the *braves* around the council fire would arouse all the fierce and cruel passions of his savage nature and make him rush on danger without a single feeling of fear. The wonderful influences of the songs of the Scald, the lays of the minstrels and the home ballads of the peasant are so well attested in history that I will only refer to them by way of illustration.

The precise character of Hebrew music is unknown, but we have abundant information as to the influence which it exerted on the popular mind and heart. From the nature of the instruments used in the Temple service the music must have been loud and shrill, but it was well adapted to the exultant and joyous Psalms of thanksgiving and praise that were chanted by the choirs of Levites and responded to by the great congregation of the people. As the choirs of Levites were numerous and well trained, and were composed of male and female singers we may well suppose that they had some knowledge of the principles of harmony, and that the various voices did not mingle discordant strains. Their glorious anthems may not have swelled through the courts and porches of the Temple in rich and varied harmonies, but we feel assured that to the devout Israelites they were as soul-stirring and heart-subduing as the sublime choruses of the *Te Deum* and the weeping melodies of the *Miserere* as they swell through the marble corridors, lengthened aisles and lofty arches of St. Peter's, and hush in profound silence all but the sobbing voices from hearts of penitent worshipers.

But all our conjectures are in vain. The Old Hebrew harps have been silent for twenty-five centuries. Since they were hung upon the willows of Babylon to catch the sighs of the moaning winds, no hand has waked their sweet and noble melodies; but the grand and glorious songs of Zion that thrilled the hearts of the old Hebrews in the age of their national pride and glory, have in after times carried messages of admonition, instruction, comfort and joy to the people of God, and they will in a coming age blend in the harmonies of the sublime anthem of universal worship as it arises from earth to heaven.

LECTURE V.

SOME OF THE EVENTS IN THE HISTORY OF THE HEBREWS WHICH CONTRIBUTED TO THEIR POETIC DEVELOPMENT.

In comparing Hebrew poetry with the poetry of other nations any one will be impressed with the fact that the Hebrew bards expressed their sublime thoughts and intense moral and spiritual emotions with remarkable force, terseness and simplicity, and illustrated them with unusually vivid and appropriate imagery. Much of their sublimity of conception was derived from Divine inspiration, but there were many natural causes well calculated to give fertility, elevation and vividness to their genius. We will consider some of these causes in this and succeeding lectures.

The early history of a nation is one of the most fertile fields of poetic thought and imagery. The genius of poesy loves to linger among those remote scenes and events over which time has cast a misty veil, mellowing what was dark and terrible into grand and beautiful imagery; just as distance throws its hazy enchantment over the rugged features of nature and softens and blends the lights and shadows and various objects which form the pleasing landscape.

In this respect the Hebrew bards possessed peculiar advantages, as they had a history extending far back into the misty regions of antiquity, and fuller of important events and thrilling incidents than the history of any other people that ever existed; and these events and incidents were continually presented to their minds with wonderful distinctness and power in the yearly celebration of their national feasts and religious ordinances.

The land in which they lived was almost as fertile and beautiful as the garden of Eden, and nearly every spot was hallowed by memories of divine blessings and by interesting historic associations. They were endowed with the warm and glowing fancy of the Orient, and were highly susceptible of grand and beautiful impressions.

We will now rapidly refer to some of the great events which necessarily gave coloring and vividness to their fancy, and first of all stands forth the sublime scenes of creation. The first chapter of Genesis furnishes the grandest historic panorama ever presented to human contemplation. In every line it bears the impress of divinity. It is the oldest record of history and the only one that gives any definite account of the origin of the earth and the creation of man. Blot it out and these great events would ever be unfathomable mysteries to mankind.

The wonderful, but still imperfect discoveries of physical science, as interpreted by infidel and undevout philosophers, have created in skeptical minds some speculative doubts as to the truthfulness of the Mosaic narrative; but no such doubts existed in the minds of the Hebrews. They were not acquainted with the "Records of the Rocks," and knew nothing of the teachings of Copernican astronomy. They looked upon the world as it appeared to their vision, and had entire confidence in the narrative of their great leader and lawgiver, who had afforded so many evidences of his supernatural wisdom and power, and his immediate converse with Jehovah.

When they read or heard the account given in their sacred book of the marvelous events of creation, with fervent faith they formed vivid conceptions of that period, when, "In the beginning God created the heaven and the earth. And the earth was without form and void, and darkness was upon the face of the deep; and the Spirit of

God moved upon the face of the waters;" and their devout minds were filled with the noblest emotions by those sublime creative words, "And God said, Let there be light." What a magnificent scene was then presented, witnessed only by God and the angels, and revealed to Moses in glorious vision. Upon the utterance of those creative words the dark waters and thick clouds which curtained the pavilion of Jehovah's secret habitation were rent asunder, and light beamed from the eternal throne and cast a flood of celestial radiance over the turbid ocean of chaos and made it glitter and gleam with golden glory.

The heart of a pious Hebrew must have been filled with feelings of the highest rapture when, with vivid mental vision, he saw, in grand succession, the unveiling scenes of the wondrous panorama of creation—when God covered Himself with light as with a garment, stretched out the heavens like a curtain, laid the beams of His chambers in the waters, made the clouds His chariots and walked upon the wings of the wind, attended by angel spirits and ministers like a flaming fire. What grand emotions must have thrilled his soul when his fancy pictured the earth as it was upheaved amid the receding waters and was covered in rapid succession with fresh verdure, bright and odoriferous flowers and with clustering vines and trees laden with luscious fruits; while the waters gathered into rushing rivers, gurgling streams, and "springs in the valleys that ran among the hills," or settled into broad and shining lakes and seas, or rolled in magnificent billows that chafed in angry murmurs on the ocean's shore, as if restive and impatient, even at Omnipotent control.

We imagine that the fourth scene in the panorama of creation would have excited, in the highest degree, the impressible and enthusiastic nature of an Oriental. When the sun seemed to come out of the gorgeous chambers of the East and slowly moved in radiant splendors up the blue arch of the firmament, dispelling the misty vapors, flooding the earth with golden light, giving a fresher verdure to grass and herb and tree, shedding richness of color and sweeter perfume upon the shining flowers, and glowing in quivering beams upon the living waters, and then, when his munificent course was run, casting a backward glance of iridescent glory upon the earth and skies which he had beautified and blessed. Then twilight moved with silent shadows over the slumberous earth, and from the gathering gloom of the coming night the little, timid, trembling stars peeped out like the twinkling eyes of the immortals from their celestial homes, and then the moon, in queenly beauty, attended by the shining planets, made the heavens "darkly, deeply and beautifully blue," and covered with soft, mellow and silvery light the objects which had just been glowing with the golden glories of the day, and then the balmy breezes and lulling voices of nature breathed their gentle and soothing melodies. We are not surprised that primeval man when he lost the knowledge of the true God should have bowed in worship to the sun and heavenly hosts, as they are grand objects and were well calculated to inspire the unenlightened child of nature with feelings of the highest adoration.

To the Hebrews who had a correct knowledge of Him who placed the sun in the firmament and guided all the heavenly hosts in their unerring and shining courses, the daily and nightly scenes which they witnessed were but manifestations of divine goodness and mercy, and while they elevated their feelings of adoration for the great creator, they were not objects of idolatrous worship. The ideas and emotions which they inspired were sublimely poetical, and the grandest and most beautiful metaphors of the Hebrew bards were derived from the gorgeous skies of their Orient clime.

We will not refer at any length to the other scenes

presented in the panorama of creation, although they are full of poetic suggestions and imagery. Then were created the monsters of the deep and the countless myriads of living creatures that moved in the waters. Then the wide expanded firmament and the vast forests of earth were filled with flying fowls, and with the singing birds that rejoiced in the instincts of life and poured forth their sweetest melodies. Then the hills and valleys were covered with numerous animals of various forms and natures that were wonderfully adapted for the purposes of their creation. Then man stood amidst the sinless bowers of Paradise, made in the image of God, but a little lower than the angels, and invested with power and dominion over every living creature of earth.

Then came the Sabbath, especially sanctified by God for rest, holiness and worship. How exceedingly beautiful must that first Sabbath have been, when God in visible glory was present in the holy temple which He had just finished, and all created things were offering sinless adoration and praise, and were listening with devout and pure raptures to the hymning harmonies of the angels. Earth was then but an outer court of the heavenly sanctuary, and life to man was fresh, joyous and immortal. No son of genius in his brightest dreams, no prophet in the hightest ecstacies of inspiration ever saw a vision of earth as gloriously beautiful as that first Sabbath which God blessed and hallowed when the work of creation was done.

It will come no more to the sin-cursed earth, but will dawn again on the Millennial morning, and then brighten into the higher radiance and glory of the eternal day in Heaven.

The fall of man which

> "Brought death into the world and all our woe,
> With loss of Eden,"

was one of the most important events in history. It was the beginning of man's sinful and sorrowful destiny. The sacred record of this event is very short, but it must have been very impressive and suggestive to the Hebrews. It filled the mind of Milton with grander imagery and more eloquent and rhythmic thoughts than were ever conceived by any other uninspired genius. What a wonderful transition for our first parents, from a condition of immortality, perfect purity, holiness and bliss, into a condition of sin, pain, labor, suffering and expectant death! Can there ever be a scene of human sorrow so full of deep and thrilling pathos as the departure from the Eden home of love, light and joy? When the streams, the trees, the flowers, the breezes and the pure angel spirits of Eden sent forth a melancholy chant of pity and farewell to Adam and Eve as with sorrowing hearts and weeping eyes they passed beneath the flaming sword of the Cherubim, into the dark world of exile, carrying with them none of the blessings of Eden, but human love, memories of joy and beauty and the blessed hope of Heaven through a Redeemer. How sad and drear and lonely must have been the first days of their exile. No angel voices cheered their drooping hearts, or with etherial melodies soothed their troubled slumbers. No more could they gather the luscious fruits which their sinless lips had tasted, and they thirsted in vain for the crystal waters that flowed by the tree of life. The flowers that bloomed in amaranthine bowers no longer delighted their sight and made them breathe delicious perfumes. The birds still sang in the bramble and brake, and in the wild woodlands, but they had lost the joyous trill with which they had once joined in the choir of the angels. The animals once so tame, so gentle, so sportive and so loving had now become estranged from man and each other. The blood of the lamb was on the fangs of the wolf, and the down of the dove was on the beak of the vulture. With crested head and quivering tongue the poisonous basilisk coiled in the pathway, the eagle screamed from his eyrie as he swooped for his prey, the fiery eye of the tiger gleamed from the jungle, and the angry roar of the lion made every living thing tremble with fear.

Altnough man lost so much by the fall still God in His infinite goodness and mercy made earth a beautiful home, and watched with loving and tender care over his erring children. Adam and Eve were soothed in their sadness by the blessed hope of redemption, and during their long and checkered lives had many days of brightness and joy, mingled with days of darkness and sorrow. These primal scenes in human history are full of beauty and poetry to us, but they must have been far more impressive to the earnest and religious Hebrews in the beautiful land which God had given to them for an inheritance.

The short fragmentary history of the antediluvian age is very suggestive of poetical thoughts to an imaginative mind. Adam was created in the image of His Maker, in the full perfection of manhood, and must have possessed extensive knowledge and wisdom, which his centuries of life enabled him to communicate to his descendants. The longevity of the antediluvian patriarchs afforded them ample time and opportunities to increase in knowledge, and improve the arts and sciences which contributed to the necessities, comforts and elegances of life. They built cities and many of them "became mighty men which were of old men of renown." Then the "sons of God" loved and wooed the beautiful daughters of men, and lived with them in wedded bliss. Then Jabal and his children pitched their tents on the green hillsides and fertile valleys, and in the midst of flocks and herds, dwelt in the quiet contentment of plenty and repose.

Then the tuneful sons of Jubal made their simple harps and pipes breathe forth sweet melodies to their astonished, delighted and rejoicing kindred. Then Tubal-Cain on his ringing anvil taught men how to form the sword and spear for angry strife, and the plow-share and pruning-hook for peaceful husbandry.

The fact is worthy of being noticed in this connection, that Lamech, the first poet of whom we have any history, was the father of Jabal, Jubal and Tubal-Cain, the inventors of the arts to which we have referred.

Pastoral life and the arts have always been associated with poetry. The song which Lamech sang to his distressed and weeping wives has been called the "song of the sword." It is the only extant antediluvian song, and was transmitted by tradition through many dark centuries and, under the direction of the Holy Spirit, was recorded by Moses. It seems to have been preserved because it was the prelude notes of the awful diapason of war and carnage, which, amid the wail of humanity, has resounded through succeeding ages. It was the first recorded song of sinful man, and recalls to our memory the facts that, at the creation of the sinless earth, "the morning stars sang together and all the sons of God shouted for joy," and the first song of the Gospel was the anthem of glory, peace and good will to men which the angels sang to the shepherds of Bethlehem.

We will not dwell longer upon the antediluvian age. With the exception of the short narrative of Moses, it has no authentic history. It has ever been and will ever be a period of mystery and conjecture. No mortal hand will ever uncover the flood-buried annals of mankind. Many traditions and legends of this age must have existed among the Hebrews and filled up omissions in their fragmentary sacred history, and must have presented vivid pictures of antediluvian patriarchal life, and produced many songs and poems which have been lost in the whelming tides of time.

No event in the history of the world produced a more profound and lasting impression upon the ancient nations than the deluge. Traditions of this event, resembling in many respects the Mosaic narrative, existed among the Chaldeans, Persians, Egyptians, Greeks and other Oriental nations, and were also found among the American Indians, the Mexicans and Peruvians, upon a distant continent, unknown to the nations of the ancient world. These traditions mingled with the religious beliefs of these nations and constituted a large ingredient in their poetical literature. We may well conclude that an event so graphically recorded by Moses, and so implicitly believed by his people, and so suggestive of terror, power and immensity, must have highly excited the fervid imagination, and stirred to the utmost depths the souls of the religious Hebrews. Even in this distant age, the short, simple and impressive narrative of Moses, enfeebled as it is by translation into our language, presents a vivid and sublime picture.

We can form only a faint conception of the thoughts and emotions which must have filled the minds and hearts of Noah and his family when shut up in the ark by the hand of God, saddened with human sorrows, but in the tranquil confidence of faith, and in security and solemn repose, they passed unharmed through the great world drama.

Universal night, as deep and dark as chaos, shrouded the earth, the windows of heaven were opened and forth came the rushing torrents and the howling storms. The fountains of the great deep were broken up, and the cruel hungry waters, in seething billows, gathered around their shrieking and defenceless victims. Loud wails of agony sounded through the terrific gloom, rising above the roar of the tempests, and grew fainter and fainter in the continuous midnight. Then was heard

> "A solitary shriek, the bubbling cry,
> Of some strong swimmer in his agony,"

and then all became still save the triumphant shouts of the winds and waves as they swept over that ocean without a shore. Long they kept their wild revels over the vast watery grave of the sinful race, and then they became obedient to the Almighty power that sent them forth on their dread mission of devastation and death; and the winds were tamed into breezes and the subdued waters rolled in playful and musical billows over the bosom of the receding ocean. The raven messenger returned not from his unweared flight; the timid dove three times sent forth upon the restless winds, at last brought an emblem of peace and good will; the mountains rose into the serene heavens amid the sunlit air, and then the purged and renovated earth smiled in fresh verdure and beauty. The smoke of the sacrifice then ascended from Noah's rude altar, and then upon the astonished vision of the late flood-voyagers shone the bow of promise in motionless calm and glorious radiance, the effulgent and benignant light of the great eye of heaven glowing on the dark bosom of the receding storm.

Some of the grandest poetry in every literature is derived from the contemplation of the ocean. Whether tortured into fury by the wintry storms or reposing in calm benignant glory beneath bright summer skies, the ocean is an emblem of vastness, dread magnificence and power, and fills the mind and heart with a sublimity of awe that is produced by no other object in the natural world. We feel that it is an image of eternity, a " glorious mirror where the Almighty's form" is almost visible, and it rolls on "fathomless and alone"

> " Time writes no wrinkle on thine azure brow
> Such as creation's dawn beheld, thou rollest now."

Yet man passes over its watery wildernesses, encounters its wild billows and reaches the safe harbors of commerce. He can measure its expanse, map out its currents, dive into its caverns and gather its hid treasures, and send the lightning bearing human thoughts over its submerged valleys and mountains. It was not so with the unknown, the illimitable and fathomless oceans of Chaos and the Deluge. If the Atlantic and Pacific, as they mingle their waters and sweep round the globe, clap their hands in fierce joy and call to each other across the continent, produce such high poetic inspirations and furnish such magnificent imagery, we may somewhat conceive the influence upon the minds and hearts of the Hebrews while contemplating in fervid thought that universal ocean that once rolled in darkness over the unformed world; or those shoreless and whelming tides upon which floated the solitary Ark bearing the remnant of the human race and moving without chart and compass under the guidance of an Omnipotent Pilot until safely anchored upon the top of lofty Ararat.

The short post-diluvian history to the time of Abraham, showing the formation of the different nations and the re-peopling of the earth by various migrations, presented many striking scenes which together with many traditions opened a wide field for the poetic fancy and speculative thought of the Hebrews.

The divine call of Abraham, accompanied with the promise that he should be the father of a great nation and in him should all the families of the earth be blessed, was the most important event in early Hebrew history. It was the genesis of that peculiar and distinctive race, and all the attendant circumstances of tribal development were well calculated to fill the hearts of their posterity with pious, patriotic and poetic feelings. We know that primal events in the histories of other peoples were fruitful sources of poetic sentiment. The Phœnecian Cecrops founded the kingdom of Attica, and the mythic stories of those early days were immortalized in Grecian art, eloquence and song. Æneas fleeing from the ruins of Troy, and after varied fortunes reaching the Lavinian shore and planting the germ of the Latin race, is the subject of Virgil's sublime epic. The landing of Hengist and Horsa and their Saxon followers on the shores of Britain is an important and poetic era in English history. The simple annals of the Pilgrim Fathers and the Christian heroism which they displayed in laying the foundations of our free civil and religious institutions kindle the genius and patriotism of the American people, thrill and renovate the heart, and have produced some of the finest eloquence and poetry in our literature.

No poet of ancient or modern times has ever drawn an ideal character equal to that of the God chosen Abraham, or in their brightest dreams of genius have conceived of scenes of pastoral quietude, contentment and repose comparable in simple beauty to those presented in the sacred history of that grand old nomadic chieftain dwelling on the wolds of Canaan. He was so just and generous in all his intercourse with his neighbors. With tender and fatherly care he watched over his obedient family and instructed them in his sublime faith and wisdom. No dreams of ambition, no longings for temporal power, no cares and anxieties about earthly wealth ever marred the quietude of his repose or disturbed the serenity of his noble spirit. In his hospitable tents the poor and strangers found a cordial welcome, and angels were sometimes his guests. He was brave and unselfish and ever ready to succor the wronged and oppressed. He possessed and always exhibited the noblest traits of human character, and well deserved his glorious destiny, as the " Friend of God," the progenitor of a great nation and the spiritual father of the faithful in all coming ages.

The histories of Isaac and Jacob, although written in simple prose, are full of the spirit and imagery of poetry. The story of Joseph is an idyl of incomparable pathos and beauty. It has won the admiration of every age, and no one who has any poetry in his soul can read it without feeling the sweetest and tenderest emotions, while his eyes are hazy with tears.

Now we come to the long sojourn in Egypt, the "land of cloudless clime and starry skies," the land of treasure, cities, pyramids, obelisks and gorgeous temples of the sun, the land of the figtree, the lotus and palm, and where the generous Nile, with its wealth of sweet waters, made a fertile garden in the desert. In the green pastures of Goshen the sons of Jacob dwelt as herdsmen and shepherds under the munificent care of their princely brother. Then came the hard bondage under the Pharaoh who knew not Joseph. Then a beautiful and wondrous child was placed by a pious mother, with love and faith, in a frail cradle upon the turbid river, and he was reared in the palaces of Egypt, and was instructed in all the wisdom of that highly cultured people. Then came the set time for Israel's deliverance. The sound of the cruel taskmaster's scourge and the supplicating cries and wails of anguish that had long ascended from the sweltering brick-fields and from the sorrowful homes of toiling and oppressed Israel, had been heard in heaven. A voice had spoken from the burning bush in Horeb, and the Midian shepherd, invested with divine power and wisdom, had returned from his mountain solitude to enter upon his mighty mission. Then commenced the grand drama of the exodus. Pharaoh would not let Israel go to serve their God, and nine times terrible judgments fell upon the people of that beautiful land. The Hebrews in their heaven-protected homes witnessed the terrific and wondrous scenes that were enacted around them. With ready obedience they consecrated their homes with the hyssop and blood of the lamb and prepared the Passover supper. With due preparation for journeying, they were eating in haste, when in the deep gloom of the midnight the startled air rang with the wild shrieks of a nation's agony, for the first-born in every Egyptian home was dead. Then came the command, "go forward," and on the desert pathway of the multitudinous host shone in blazing radiance the moving pillar of fire. No people ever had such a commencement to their national destiny, and these initial scenes were but the beginning of wonders. Toilworn and weary with three days' march they reached the sea. The rapid tread of Pharaoh's advancing hosts and the noise of the chariot wheels were heard behind, and before them were the rolling and leaping waters. Their hearts were filled with fear and their mouths with bitter murmurings, but their undaunted leader stretched forth his rod over the swelling waves, and a strong east wind, like a mighty hand, rolled up the billows into walls as firm as adamant, and timid Israel went down on dry ground into the bosom of the deep and received the baptism of the sea, and when the morning came they stood in safety and freedom on the farther shore, and the pursuing Egyptians were swallowed by the waves returning in their strength.

Jehovah "hath triumphed gloriously; the horse and his rider hath He thrown into the sea." Then from millions of rejoicing hearts swelled out a grand song of triumph over the desert and wild waters, and was echoed by the timbrels and choruses of Miriam and the women of rescued Israel. This was the first day of Israel's accomplished freedom, and the first act of their national life was a grand triumphal and thanksgiving song, which seemed to consecrate them as Jehovah's earthly musicians and poets.

Then commenced the stern discipline of the desert to prepare them for their higher destiny as a religious nation—a nation of priests holy unto the Lord. They tasted the bitter waters of Marah and murmured. With glad hearts they pitched their tents by the wells and palm trees of Elim. With astonished gaze they looked upon the dewy manna gleaming in the morning light. Then they fought with Amalek under the banner of Jehovah-Nissi. Then they saw sweet waters gushing from the rock of Horeb and in limpid coolness flowing along their hot and dusty desert pathway. Then, in the deep sublimity of reverential awe, they stood beside trembling Sinai, and from its summit, mantled in thick clouds illumined with lightnings, they heard Jehovah pronounce His inexorable law.

> "The terrors of that awful day, though past,
> Have on the tide of time great glory cast."

Every night when the Hebrews retired to rest they saw the pillar of fire blazing above the camp, and when they woke in the morning the first object that met their view was the pillar of cloud illumined with the roseate light of the dawn. In the midst of the encamping hosts stood the gorgeous Tabernacle, the dwelling place of Jehovah, covering the Ark of the Covenant, the winged Cherubim and the fadeless Shechinah. The giving of the law and the consecration of the Tabernacle completed the organization of the nation, and we believe that the first act of their completed national life was the singing of the ninetieth Psalm—the song of Moses, "The Psalm of Eternity," the grand Te Deum, which through the ages has given consolation and joy to the living and the dying, and irradiated the memories and graves of the dead. We will not trace the history of the wilderness wanderings. After forty years of wondrous events Israel crossed the Jordan "dry shod" and pitched their tents in the beautiful land of Promise, their forefathers home. With such a varied and marvellous history gleaming with supernatural glory, and continued through eventful centuries, is it to be a matter of astonishment that Israel was a nation of bards, some of whose songs and sublime poems have so long thrilled the hearts of mankind and are destined to be the joy of the whole earth.

LECTURE VI.

Messianic Hopes.—Climate and Scenery of Palestine.

Although the Hebrews had a grand and glorious history they had national and religious hopes still more glorious. The golden age of the heathen poets was in the past, but the Hebrew bards, while not unmindful of the past, were inspired with brighter expectations of the future; and they eagerly longed for the coming glories of the expected morning when the Sun of Righteousness would arise with healing in His wings. The genius of the Greek and Roman poets was kindled by contemplating the myths and traditions of fabulous and heroic ages; but the souls of the Hebrew bards glowed with fervid enthusiasm, as, with the vivid visions of prophetic hope, they looked through the long vista of the future and saw, surrounded with triumphal splendors, the glorious King who would rule His people Israel; who would establish His throne on Mount Zion, and have dominion over the whole earth. That then the haughty and cruel Assyrian and Chaldean would be trodden under the feet of the conqueror, and the wild sons of Ishmael and Edom would bring tribute to the children of Jacob.

With what a glorious burst of lyric rapture did Isaiah picture the future of Jerusalem—the type of the Church of God,—"Arise, shine, for thy light is come and the glory of the Lord is risen upon thee. And the Gentiles shall come to thy light and kings to the brightness of thy rising." "Whereas, thou has been forsaken and hated, so that no man went through thee; I will make thee an eternal excellency; a joy of many generations." "The sun no more shall be thy light by day; neither for brightness shall the moon give light unto thee, but the Lord shall be unto thee an everlasting light, and thy God, thy glory."

Such thoughts, feelings and bright Messianic hopes must necessarily have given a rich and gorgeous coloring to the fancy of the Hebrews, as they entered into the faith and feelings of the entire nation. Tney stirred the languid blood and kindled with beaming light the eyes of the old patriarch as he sat at his tent door at eventide and mused in holy contemplation upon the promised blessings of Jehovah, and watched the sun softly sinking behind the purple shadows of the hills to rise again and gild with glory the portals of the morning.

Such thoughts and hopes were ever present with the Priests and Levites, and hallowed their ministrations; and made luminous with the light of faith all the mystic rites of the ceremonial service. They added a heavenly radiance to the smile of love which played upon the face of the young Hebrew mother as she soothed her beauteous first-born son to quiet slumbers; and then the yearning hope for the Promised One made her bow, with almost adoration, beside the innocent and sleeping child.

On the lonely Judean hill, when the midnight had hushed all nature in solemn stillness and repose, the devout shepherd, as he tended his sleeping flock, and, in holy contemplation, gazed upon the deep blue skies, glowing with the emblazonry of orient stars, often had a more glorious mental vision of a coming time when the Expected One would appear as the Great Shepherd of Israel, and gather His spiritual flocks into the secure folds of His love, guide them gently and safely through the dark and dangerous valleys of earth; and then lead them to the green pastures on the everlasting hills of heaven, to drink the crystal waters of the river of life.

The sublimest poetic raptures thrilled the hearts and illumined the imagination of the ancient prophets when in vivid vision they saw "The Prince of Peace, The Wonderful, The Councellor;" and their rapt and inspired souls heard some of the symphonies of the Seraphim, as they poured forth magnificent anthems of celestial joy and praise.

The expectation of the Messiah was coeval with the fall of man. It was awakened by the blessed promise that accompanied the primal curse of labor, sorrow and death. It existed among all the ancient nations as a dim and shadowy ideal conception, the yearning of the sad heart of humanity after some future good; some great deliverer from the ills and woes of life. With the Hebrews it was a real, vital and intense hope of individual happiness and national greatness and glory in the near future; and it cast a coruscating and consecrating glow upon all the proud achievements and memories of the past. It was a perpetual halo, shedding its light around their hearts and homes, and brightened all their ideas of the true, the beautiful and the good.

We can scarcely be surprised to find that such a living hope greatly influenced Hebrew history, and is often found glowing in the highest strains of impassioned bards.

We believe that it is generally conceded that the climate and scenery of a country have much influence in developing the imaginative faculties of a poeple. There is no fact better established in the history of literature. There seems to be a peculiar combination of natural causes and objects necessary to produce the highest poetic inspiration. The genius of poesy seems to dwell only in lands where nature is wild, bright, joyous and beautiful; where she sings her *jubilates* on the sunny hills or in the shaded valleys, and the winds, storms and cataracts hymn their sublime *te deums* in mountain temples. The broad and fertile valleys of the Euphrates and Nile, although the birth-places of the arts, sciences and speculative philosophies, and were covered with rich and splendid cities, the homes of a highly civilized people, gave no immortal poetry to the ancient world. While Greece, filled with picturesque mountains and vales, with whispering groves and musical streams, surrounded by sun-bright seas dotted with emerald isles, was the favorite home of the Muses. The same may be said of Italy, lying beneath the shadows of the Alps, interspersed with shining lakes, rushing streams and laughing rills, intersected with the forest-clad Apennines and washed on either shore by the blue and gleaming waters of the Mediterranean. We might present similiar parallels of countries in modern times, but the fact as to the influences of climate and scenery is so well established that it needs no further argument or illustration. The contemplation of nature in its grand and beautiful aspects seems to expand the soul and give boldness and vigor to the flights of the imagination. From the contemplation of the wonders and beauties of the natural world man, even without divine revelation, may form a vivid conception of a Deity.

In looking upon the world, full of so many objects of usefulness, goodness and beauty, so skillfully adjusted and arranged in order and harmony, all beaming in the magnificence of light, the human mind is filled with the grand idea that God is in His glorious temple and is worthy of the adoration and praise of His creatures. The ancient pagans could see in all the natural objects which surrounded them motion, activity, life, order, harmony and beauty, which they attributed to the influence of different divinities, and thus was formed their polytheistic belief, which was refined, elevated and beautified by the skillful production of the architect, painter and sculptor, but more than all by the creative genius of the poet.

The Hebrews looked upon nature with the eye of a nobler faith. They did not understand the natural laws and principles which the investigations of modern scientists have so largely discovered, but they believed that all the varied objects of nature were connected by a general plan and were under the constant control of an Omniscient, Omnipresent and Omnipotent Being, the sovereign of their nation and their personal God.

If we will take a rapid survey of the land of the Hebrews we will find that it was possessed of that peculiar combination of natural objects and historic associations favorable to high poetic development. No where was there a country on the earth which had a more delightful climate and presented a scenery more grand, beautiful and picturesque than the ancient land of Palestine. Its mountains, hills and plains of different elevations, and its ravines and valleys gave it the diversity of temperature and the varied vegetation of nearly every clime, from perpetual winter to the luxuriance of tropical summer. In the time of the ancient Hebrews the country was exceedingly fertile, and was covered with forests and groves of cedar, olive, myrtle, palm, terebinth, oak and accacia and various other trees, furnishing cool and refreshing shades, and they were musical with birds of sweetest song and richest plumage, and were fragrant with breezes that bore on their odoriferous wings the balmy treasures of the East.

The country was also in a state of high cultivation. Agriculture was not only the principle business of the people, but it was to them a delightful occupation. The fertile valleys, plains and hillsides smiled beneath the hand of careful and intelligent industry, and filled the barns and storehouses with plenty. Even rocky ridges and deep declivities were clothed with fruitfulness and verdure by the cheerful and diligent culture of the husbandman. In the midst of these rich fields, green pastures, blooming gardens and fruitful vineyards and olive groves, there were shady glens and picturesque ravines where nature reigned in undisturbed dominion, and displayed in varied forms her wild luxuriant beauties, inviting the toil-worn and weary to quietude and repose.

Palestine was indeed a paradise land. It was surrounded by mountains, deserts and seas—the fortresses which Jehovah had placed as defences to guard the sacred heritage. It also abounded with perennial springs and clear sweet brooks and rills that ran among the valleys and the hills, and it bloomed with many-colored wild flowers, those little but eloquent messengers of God, those gentle children of the morning light bearing fragrant censers jewelled with the sunshine and the dew.

Natural causes produced an atmosphere more transparent than that of Italy, which gave a crysteline lustre to the azure skies and a clearer radiance to the orient sun, and at night made the stars appear like gleaming "isles of light" in "a deep blue ocean hung on high," or to the more spiritual fancy, like oriel windows in the sapphire dome of heaven, emitting the effulgence of the inner celestial glory.

Although Palestine was so highly favored with the beauty, magnificence and rich bounty of nature, it was not exempt from those various natural causes which in other lands produce feelings of awe and terror and inspire sublime poetic thoughts and imagery. The Hebrews often felt the convulsive throes of the earthquake, saw the fierce and glittering lightning and heard the deep-voiced thunder as it marshaled the dread cohorts of the storm.

They witnessed the devastations of the whirlwinds and of the turbid torrents that rushed madly from the hills over the fertile valleys. Swarms of locusts desolated their vineyards and fruitful fields; beasts of prey prowled around the folds and pastures of their flocks and herds; and "the pestilence that walketh in darkness and wasteth at noonday" sometimes filled their homes with suffering and sorrow. On the Southwestern border of the land was the gloomy sea that ever reminded them of the sinful cities of the plain and Jehovah's terrific judgment. Around it was a desolate wilderness, filled with overhanging precipices, rocky pinnacles and deep and dark gorges—fit symbols of the valley and shadow of death. We know that from such scenes, occurences and objects the Hebrew bards derived some of their sublimest thoughts and many of their most striking similes and metaphors.

We will now briefly describe some of the most prominent features and scenes of the country which God selected, enriched and adorned as the home of His Chosen People. There was Mount Tabor, rising like a monarch among the fertile hills of Galilee, crowned with evergreen verdure and mantled with graceful vines. At its foot was Esdraelon, the battle-ground of nations, spreading like a vast embroidered carpet fresh from nature's loom, and surrounded with the amphitheatre of the blue mountains of Israel. To the north was Lebanon with its towering cedars, forming the pillared palaces of the storm, and down its rocky sides in continuous currents were flowing clear, cool and glittering streams from glacier fountains. Just beyond a deep, broad and fertile valley, filled with splendid cities and enriched by skillful-cultivation, stood Mount Hermon,

> " Whose head in wintry grandeur towers,
> And whitens with eternal sleet,
> While summer, in a vale of flowers,
> Is sleeping rosy at his feet."

From its summit were seen the giant structures of Hazor, the wild and rugged mountain pass of Hamath, and the far famed rivers of Damascus, beautifying and refreshing a garden plain resting like an island of verdure in an ocean desert. On the north-western border of Palestine was sweet and dear Genesareth. With lavish beauty nature seemed to have adorned her for her hallowed history. Sometimes she reposed in waveless calm and brightly smiled as she received the warm, loving kiss of the sun, and with silver-like mirror reflected in mingled tints of saphire, emerald and gold, images of the green mountains and blue unfathomable skies. Then her gently swelling billows joined in the sports of the playful winds, and then she writhed in agony and rage when her peaceful realms were invaded by the fierce legions of the tempest. Through her bosom flowed the sacred Jordan, so memorable in Hebrew history. It, too, had its varying moods. Sometimes swollen into a torrent by the melting snows of Hermon it swept in rolling tides over the adjacent valley, then in smooth and limpid current it glided in musical gladness beneath the shadowing palms and by the verdant and blooming shores, and then in joyous freedom rushed along the winding rapids and leaped in thundering cascades of foaming splendors.

Beyond were the stately oaks and the extended pastures of Bashan; the prosperous cities and balmy groves of Gilead; the lofty summit of Nebo—the mount of glorious vision and the sepulchre of the great lawgiver, and there the dark, stern mountains of Moab stood like grim and relentless sentinels over the gloomy grave of the sinful cities of the plain. To the south the mountains of Edom, indented with their rocky peaks the blue rim of the horizon and overlooked that "great and terrible wilderness" which had been the scene of so many astounding miracles, and the place of Israel's long wandering and sufferings before they reached "the goodly land" of plenty and repose. In nearer vision and beautified by contrast were the hills and vales of Judah, undulating like the waves of ocean, clothed with the fruitfulness and verdure of a genial clime, covered with bleating flocks and lowing herds, where the lilies of the valley bloomed by perennial fountains, where grew in purple clusters the luscious grapes of Eshcol, and where the sweetest honey was ever dripping from the fissures of the rocks. Amidst these scenes of pastoral beauty and picturesque loveliness rose Jerusalem, "The Holy City," radiant with architectural splendors, surrounded by blooming gardens and embowered in groves of the richest foliage, consecrated by so many glorious memories and hopes, and encircled by the sacred mountains, the poetic emblems of Jehovah's protecting presence. To the west was the solemn-sounding and mysterious sea, spreading beneath cloudless skies far beyond the limits of vision, burnished with the golden light of the orient sun, and ever rolling its restless waves upon the shores where bloomed the "Roses of Sharon" and smiled the green pastures and rich gardens of Carmel.

In every part of this beautiful, luxuriant and sacred land there were terraced slopes covered with thriving villages, towns and cities, and quiet hamlets and cottages nestled in fertile valleys beneath shadowy hills—all the happy homes of a people rejoicing in the blessings of health, plenty and freedom.

This was the " Land of Promise," more beautiful than a poet's or painter's brightest dream, for it was blessed by the smile and hallowed by the special beneficence of Jehovah. What land so meet a nurse for poetic child?

LECTURE VII.

History and Traditions of Paradise. The Sabbath. The Manners and Customs of the Hebrews.

We concluded our last lecture with a brief description of the Land of Promise. From this subject the transition is easy and natural to the consideration of the influence exerted upon the Hebrews by the history and belief of Paradise.

Among all the ancient pagan nations there existed a traditionary idea of a lost Paradise. This idea seemed to pervade the whole earth like an invisible seraph from Eden, breathing sweet harmonies and filling the human heart with shadowy visions of the distant past, when primeval man lived in a condition of simplicity innocence, contentment and blissful repose; in a home of abounding plenty and exquisite picturesque beauty; always bright with serene summer skies and balmy with delicious odors; where existence required no toil, and life was unmarred by disappointment and sorrow, and was not darkened by expectations of death and the gloom of the grave.

This idea was largely intermingled with the early history, traditions and religious beliefs of the various nations of antiquity, and was a fruitful germ of their poetry and art. It gave rise to the beautiful fables of the golden age, and of the gardens of the Hesperides, and numerous other myths with which genius enriched the immortal pages of classic literature.

If we had no truthful history of Paradise we might readily conclude that an idea so universally prevalent was derived from some reality which existed in prehistoric ages, and was not a mere ideal conception of the human mind. If, then, an idea transmitted by tradition through the revolutions of centuries and enveloped in the shadows of fable had such suggestive and creative influence upon the literature of so many different nations we may well imagine that the Mosaic account of the garden of Eden, which was implicitly believed by the Hebrews to be not only a truthful but a sacred narrative, must have highly excited and developed their imaginative faculties. They were truly Orientals, the descendants of Shem, and possessed in a high degree the characteristics of that susceptible and imaginative race who sought habitations towards the rising sun, and who in idolatry worshiped the shining heavenly hosts.

Sweet to the aged and care-worn man are the remembrances of childhood days that awaken new pulses of life in his feebly throbbing heart and bring a light of joy to his eyes enfeebled with age and dimmed by tears. Sweet to the erring and friendless outcast are the bright visions that visit him in dreams and carry him back over sorrowing years to a happy home of innocence, purity and love. Sweet to the exile are memories of the fatherland from which he had wandered far away over the mountains and the seas. But sweeter, dearer, holier to the pious Hebrew were the memories of Eden, the beautiful and sacred land of purity, plenty and repose—the sinless home of his first parents, where they had dwelt in innocence and bliss in frequent communion with Jehovah and the angels. It was not only a source of holy memories, but it was a fountain of poetic inspiration, from which flowed a crystal Pactolus enriched with golden sands. To us the glories of the earthly Eden are dimmed by the more effulgent light that beams from the Gospel and gives us brighter faith visions of the heavenly home. To the early Hebrews these sweet and hallowing memories of a lost Paradise, together with the promise of a Messiah were only faintly suggestive of a future home of the soul.

Although the teachings of the earlier books of the Old Testament on this subject are dim, shadowy and typical, yet the New Testament distinctly shows us how the ancient Hebrews understood their own sacred writings in regard to a future existence. With the aid of the New Testament we are able to comprehend the import of the ceremonial types and symbolic images of the Old Testament dispensation, which prefigured the doctrines of the atonement, redemption, regeneration and a blessed immortality. At first these great truths were seen only in the dim twilight, and in the after days of the prophets and Psalmists they increased into the brighter radiance of the dawn, and then burst into the effulgent splendor of the morning, when Christ rose from the dead and "brought life and immortality to light" through the Gospel, which has irradiated the world with the glorious day of Christianity.

Shadowy and dim as were the conceptions of the Hebrews of that religion which beams in the fullness of light and purity from the New Testament, yet they were highly suggestive of poetic thought. They inspired Job with some of his sublimest rhapsodies, they were the themes of many of the most glorious Psalms, and often glowed with peculiar brightness in the lyric raptures of the prophets. They cheered the Israelites in captivity, and were the Shechinah glory of the second temple. They were carried by the Jews to all parts of the Alexandrian empire, and influenced in some degree the literature, philosophy and even the religions of the ancient nations. The doctrine of the immortality of the soul was taught in the schools of Athens, Alexandria and Antioch, and it was incorporated into the philosophy and sublime monotheistic faith of Zoroaster. Everywhere and in every language it found a response in the human soul and gave inspiration to the highest poetic genius.

In this department of religious literature the minds and hearts of Christian poets have been illumined by the inspiration of Christian faith. In the whole range of human contemplation there is no subject so suggestive of beautiful thoughts and pure and holy emotions as the Christian hope of Heaven. Around this hope cluster all the pure joys of life, the sweet memories of the past, and the earnest aspirations of the soul. With this hope, life is not a continuity of sorrow and care, a dreary funeral march to the grave, but a solemn and pleasant pilgrimage to a better land, the home of unending love, unalloyed bliss, exceeding beauty and everlasting rest. There with friends and loved ones, with saints and martys, with Apostles, Prophets, Psalmists and Patriarchs, with Cherubim and Seraphim, with Jesus and with God the Father, the redeemed souls can enter upon an eternal life of progressive development, where, ever beholding the glory of the Lord, they are changed into the same image from glory to glory.

The Sabbath is properly regarded as an earthly type of Heaven, and we will now proceed to consider the influence of that sacred institution upon Hebrew development. The holy observance of the Sabbath by the Hebrews contributed materially to their moral and intellectual advancement, and to the preservation and elevation of their national poetry. This institution was established in Eden when primeval man was sinless and perfect in physical and moral organization. Even then divine wisdom and goodness deemed such an institution necessary for the welfare and happiness of man. It seems to have floated like a waif from that beautiful morning land of its birth down the dark stream of the ages, through the antediluvian period and the times of the patriarchal church.

When God selected and set apart a peculiar people as the special depositaries of His sacred oracles, and formed them into a nation, He reaffirmed this divine appointment, and defined and imposed duties and obligations in the Decalogue proclaimed from Sinai. From that time to the present day the Sabbath has been more or less observed, and has conferred numberless civil, domestic and religious blessings upon mankind. Human experience has shown that one day in seven for repose and especial spiritual exercises is as essential for the healthful, physical, moral and intellectual development of man as food is necessary for the sustenance of the body. Individuals and nations who fail to enjoy this divine blessing, and to obey this imperative law of nature, are subject to sure demoralization and decline.

The Jews after the captivity became a nation of Puritans, and made the Sabbath a day of penance, self-denial and gloom by the ritualistic formulas and ceremonials required in its observance.

Among the old Hebrews it was a cheerful and happy day, spent in physical rest from daily toil, in duties of charity and mercy, in joyous thanksgivings to God, and in the pleasant association of friends and neighbors.

Those who were conveniently near witnessed the unusually splendid and imposing services of the sanctuary, and those who were too remote for this high privilege gathered round the prophets and elders and heard recitals of the wondrous history and hopes of their nation. These assemblies were usually enlivened and cheered with instrumental music, songs and the sacred dance. All their observances of this sacred day tended to excite pleasing and elevating emotions that made melody in their hearts. Thus one day in seven their physical energies were refreshed and their moral natures elevated and spiritualized, and they learned to associate ideas of the holy and the beautiful which formed the true spirit of poetry.

We may in some degree form an idea of the hallowing and elevating influence of the Sabbath upon this ancient and imaginative people by considering the effect which the Christian Sabbath has produced upon the advancement of modern civilization and the enjoyments of mankind.

In the Apostolic age the first day of the week, the day of the Resurrection, was ordained as the Christian Sabbath, and was righteously observed by the primitive Church in the time of its simplicity, purity and holiness. During the mediæval apostasy of the Romish hierarchy the Sabbath was observed, not as a holy day, but as a holiday, and was generally spent in pompous displays and in festivity and mirth. Even the early Reformers did not regard the religious observance of the Sabbath as obligatory upon Christians, as they believed it to be an institution which had passed away with the Jewish dispensation. But the Puritans who gave civil and religious liberty to England restored the sanctity of the Sabbath and established it as an institution indispensable to pure Christianity. The rigid and unnecessary observances which they imposed have passed away before a more enlightened and spiritual faith. The Christian Sabbath since the days of the Long Parliament has moved on with English constitutional freedom and enlightenment in their rapid expansion and advancement, and it is now regarded by Protestants in Great Britain and the United States as a divine and beneficent institution. We feel the inspirations of the Sabbath consecrated by the holiest memories and associations and illumined with glorious hopes. The tones of the Church bells ring out so joyously, waking the softest and purest melodies of the heart, as they summon the old and the young, the rich and the poor, to enter the gates of the Lord's house with thanksgiving and His courts with praise, and there from holy altars re-kindle in their hearts the fires of faith, hope and charity.

The Sabbath sunshine seems to fall with soft and hallowing radiance upon the quiet churchyard where sleep the loved and pious dead, and glows like celestial light irradiating the tomb. It reminds the Christian heart of those bright hopes that make the grave the shining gateway of heaven where welcoming angels receive the redeemed spirit and bear it to that blissful home "where the wicked cease from troubling and the weary are at rest."

The Hebrew Sabbath was commemorative of the perfected work of creation. The Christian Sabbath is commemorative of a far grander event, the perfected work of redemption, when the bright hope of immortality was assured to man by the resurrection of our Saviour. One was especially sanctified for the adoration of sinless man in Eden, and was afterwards established as a day of rest and holiness for the chosen people. The other is an emblem of the day of everlasting rest and praise of the redeemed in heaven. In both we find elements suggestive of the sweetest and most sublime poetry.

Among the Hebrews the Sabbath was not only a religious institution but exerted a marked and peculiar influence upon their civil and political economy. It gave rise to other Sabbatical observances. Every seventh year the land had rest from culture and kept a "Sabbath for the Lord." During that year the spontaneous productions of the fields and vineyards were dedicated by law to the use of the poor and the sojourning stranger. Then all debts were suspended, all secular business discontinued and the beasts of burden and the slaves had release from toil. The unusual productiveness of the previous year filled their barns and storehouses with overflowing abundance, and every heart was made glad with the enjoyment of plenty, which was a special blessing from the Lord.

The seventh sabbatical year was the great year of Jubilee, when freedom from debts and slavery was proclaimed throughout the whole land, and every Hebrew was restored to his patrimonial inheritance, and the exile returned with songs and rejoicing to the home which he had left in poverty and sorrow. This time was looked for with longing expectation and with the fondest and dearest hopes by all who were saddened by sorrow and misfortune, or oppressed with poverty and slavery. The Jubilee was the birth period of a new domestic, tribal and national life, and the whole year was spent in festivity and rejoicing. On the tenth day of the seventh month—the great Day of Atonement—the silver trumpets of the sanctuary were blown beside the brazen altar to proclaim the year of Jubilee. The sounds were heard by Levites placed at convenient distances on elevated positions, who also blew signal trumpets. Thus the clear and ringing notes of the trumpets of Jubilee, started from the sanctuary, and seemed to leap from hill top to hill top waking gladsome echos among the valleys and carrying a joyous message to every heart and home in Israel. I will not further consider the objects of this institution or the influences which it exerted upon the religious, social and political welfare of the people. It was designed by God for wise and beneficent purposes, and greatly promoted the perpetuity, prosperity and happiness of the people. It must have had great influence in developing the purest and noblest virtues. A year so full of blessings must have inspired feelings of the profoundest thankfulness and gratitude to God, and the highest love and devotion to country, and filled the mind with pleasing and elevated thoughts that often swelled into the glad and beautiful language of poetry. The sweetest and holiest emotions that ever thrill the heart are those that spring from love for God, for country and for home, and they have produced rich and immortal poetry in every literature. These influences and emotions operated powerfully upon the Hebrews, and the effects can be traced through their whole history to their latest posterity.

The manners and customs of the Hebrews in social and domestic life furnish strong evidence of their moral and intellectual advancement and poetic temperament. They were the most kindhearted, polite and accomplished people of their times. They were remarkably fond of social intercourse, and their manners were always frank, amiable and refined. Their domestic life was full of parental, filial and conjugal love and tenderness. The patriarchal customs of their ancestors which they observed, prepared them in early life for the faithful and affectionate observance of the fifth commandment of the Decalogue, and no people in any age more fully venerated the crown of gray hairs and honored the face of the old man. Like all oriental races they showed a courteous and liberal hospitality to strangers. They were kind and generous to the poor and friendless and exhibited the most sympathetic benevolence to widows and the fatherless. They were lenient and humane to their servants and even their domestic animals were objects of their gentle and protecting care. In their ordinary home life they were frugal, cheerful and industrious, and not eager and grasping after gain and wealth. They were, however, fond of festive enjoyments and at such times were disposed to indulge in pomp and magnificence. The toilets of the Hebrew ladies on such occasions were especially costly and elegant, and this feminine taste had increased to such extravagance in the days of the prophets as to call forth their expostulations and severest censures. In this place I will refer only to the social and domestic festivals of the Hebrews in the course of ordinary life.

A marriage was always celebrated with beautiful and appropriate ceremonies. The procession from the home of the bride to the house of the bridegroom was witnessed by a large crowd of kindred, friends and neighbors, and was peculiarly attractive and imposing. It was led by a band of well trained musicians who made the soft evening air vibrate with the blended melodies of instrumental music and joyous song. The bridegroom was accompanied by a number of companions of his own age, and all were dressed in princely elegance. Young and beautiful virgins, arrayed in costly wedding garments, surrounded the blushing bride, and bore in their hands brightly burning lamps filled with fragrant oil and shining like a halo of stars in the gathering twilight. The long flowing hair of the bride was surmounted by a nuptial crown—a chaplet of fresh evergreens and odorous flowers—arranged by a mother's hand. Her raiment of needle work was richly embroidered with threads of gold and precious stones, was perfumed with myrrh, cassia and aloes, and was bound with a jeweled girdle. Over all hung in quivering translucent folds a snow white veil, enshrining in purity her graceful form and her youthful innocence and loveliness. As the procession approached the house of the bridegroom another company of virgins, adorned with rich festal costumes, came forth in the airy and graceful movements of the dance, bearing garlands of flowers and swinging newly trimmed and shining lamps, and with the gladsome songs of hail and welcome they mingled in the advancing train and entered into the brightly lighted hall of the marriage supper. Such a scene of joy and beauty must have charmed all beholders and made their hearts jubilant with tender emotions and melody.

The marriage feast usually lasted for seven days, but its innocent gladness and merriment never resulted in sinful indulgences and exhausting dissipation. Marriage is often referred to by the Psalmists and the Prophets, and was the subject of the beautiful "song of songs," written by the wise king of Israel. In a subsequent age it was especially honored and sanctified by the first miracle of our Saviour, and furnished illustrations in several of His touching and instructive parables. The marriage union was used as an appropriate symbol to represent the loving and tender union of Christ with His Church.

The birth of children was always an occasion of festivity, but the birthday of the first-born son was usually celebrated with the highest munificence and gladness, for the hearts of the parents were filled with thankfulness and holy joy, as the event was associated with glorious Messianic hopes. The enjoyments of the domestic festivals of the Hebrews were not confined to the immediate kindred and friends of a family but were extended with a generous hospitality to all neighbors and even strangers. In the peaceful and prosperous days of the commonwealth and monarchy there was scarcely a week in any community that was not enlivened with some festive scene, and such exciting demonstrations of joyfulness must have inspired the imagination and produced songs of love and happiness which have passed away with those olden times.

The festive scenes of primitive life contributed greatly to poetic development in other nations. They seem to have furnished the seed germs of poetry from which national literatures have sprung. These inspiring influences can be distinctly traced in the literary remains of the Greeks and Romans; they still have a living power in Italy and Germany and sunny, joyous France, and they produced much of the ballad minstrelsy of Scotland. They have enshrined in song memories of the halcyon days of merry old England; and when we hear the sweet minstrel melodies of Erin that once sounded at festive boards and in cottage homes in that land of song and old romance, we can but regret that

> "The harp that once through Tara's halls
> The soul of music shed,
> Now hangs as mute on Tara's walls
> As if that soul were fled."

The season of harvest, that lasted seven weeks, from the Passover to Pentecost, was a continuous festival in the whole land. The joyous songs of cheerful reapers, merry maidens and gleeful children were heard in every field and filled the air with delightsome melody. The grateful poor gathered the corners of the fields and the gleanings among the sheaves, and with gladsome voices joined in the "Song of the Harvest Home." The dusty threshing floor presented a scene of hilarity and mirth, and even the unmuzzled ox, in the contentment of appeased appetite, with nimble tread performed his arduous labors.

In the fall of the year came the vintage, which lasted about two months. The vineyards resounded with songs and instrumental music, and the cheerful laborers, without feelings of weariness, gathered the purple clusters and trod the foaming winepresses. The times of the harvest and vintage were also seasons of universal thankfulness and gratitude to Jehovah for His bounties; and the hearts of the people, rejoicing at the prospects of plenty, overflowed with love and kindness towards each other.

I know that I need not refer to the abundant evidence furnished in the history of literature to show the influence which rural and pastoral scenes has exerted in developing the poetic genius of a people. Such scenes have ever been the fruitful sources of inspiration for the poet. I may here appropriately quote the language of Emmerson, addressed to the poet: "Wherever snow falls, or water flows, or birds fly; wherever day and night meet in the twilight; wherever the blue heaven is hung with clouds or sown with stars; wherever are forms with transparent boundaries; wherever are outlets in celestial space; wherever is danger and awe and love, there is beauty as plenteous as rain shed for thee, and though thou should walk the world over thou shall not be able to find a condition inopportune and ignoble."

Many of the Hebrew people had their homes in walled towns and cities, that they might afford mutual protection and have means of safe and ready defence against the predatory incursions of robbers and marauders from neighboring peoples. This condition of mutual dependence tended greatly to strengthen the bonds of social and political union, and furnished opportunities of frequent association which fostered the kindly feelings of brotherhood and increased general intelligence. In times of peace the entire population of every city met morning and evening at the gates. This was usually the time and place of social gatherings and of business transactions; and it was also the time and place when the ordinary city courts were held. The judges were always present and ready to hear, adjust and determine disputes and legal controversies between citizens. This convenient, cheap and speedy administration of justice prevented long, vexatious and expensive litigation, and preserved the harmony and good order of the community.

On a cool, bright and balmy morning, as the refreshed, cheerful and industrious people went out of the gates to labor in the adjacent gardens, fields, vineyards and pasture grounds, they exchanged kindly greetings and many a pleasant look and word. In the evening, as they returned from their daily toil to seek the rest and refreshment of home, they paused at the gate to witness and often to participate in the pleasures of social intercourse.

In that orient clime there was no time that was so full of calm joyousness and exquisite beauty as the evening, when the sun in regal splendor and with parting benisons was closing the portals of the day. The heat and burden of toil was ended, and man and all nature felt the soft and lulling influences of the mystic hour. Gorgeous skies were resting on the purple hills and the verdant landscape was burnished with golden light that was slowly fading into the mellow, then dim, then dusky twilight. Then the soft evening air, as it whispered lullabies in liquid melodies, was sweetly redolent with the breath of the clustering vines; and the sleeping flowers and the wild thyme were giving out their fragrance to the dew. With gentle steps the bleating flocks and lowing herds were seeking their accustomed folds; the birds had sung their vesper hymns, and with twittering joy were nestling in their leafy homes; the plains and valleys, near and far, curtained with the mysteries of shadow, were sinking into solemn stillness and repose; and the timidly twinkling stars were marshaling for their serene march over the celestial fields, and were shedding their soft and tremulous light over the slumberous earth. There was no time when the heart would swell with sweeter, purer and holier emotions, and the mind be filled with higher thoughts and brighter fancies. The associations of the Hebrews at such times and under such circumstances must have greatly advanced their mental, moral and spiritual culture and developed their poetic genius.

LECTURE VIII.

Political Freedom. National Unity. The Religion of the Hebrews.

The political freedom of the Hebrews may well be considered as an important element in their poetic development. The renowned freedom of Greece and Rome exerted a highly developing influence upon their literature and civilization, although it was only enjoyed by a small class of citizens, while the great mass of the people were sunk in poverty and slavery. Those nations never recognized the facts that personal freedom is the gift of God, the common birthright of all mankind, and that all just government is founded upon the consent of the governed.

The government established by Moses was a theocratic republic, founded upon an express covenant freely made by the people with Jehovah; and all Hebrews were invested with equal civil and political rights, and had a representative voice in the enactment of laws regulating their civil policy. The several tribes were independent republics, and each had a local government with an executive, legislative and judicial department, administered by officers freely chosen by the people. These independent republics were formed into a federal nation by a general government which regulated the duties and relations of the several tribes, and was paramount in its powers over all matters pertaining to the general welfare. The system of local and appellate courts established by Moses were remarkably well adapted for a convenient, cheap, speedy and impartial administration of justice.

The Hebrews were the first free nation of antiquity, and both in their commonwealth and monarchy established and observed those enlightened principles of civil liberty, constitutional government and social order which have entered so largely into the governments of modern Christian nations, and which have been so splendidly developed in England and America by the Anglo-Saxon race.

The Hebrews were not only freemen in whom rested the sovereignty of the State, but they were all landowners and freeholders, and their estates were so entailed as to descend in perpetual succession. Under the Mosaic laws lands could not be aliened for a longer time than the next ensuing year of Jubilee, and were then restored to the original owners or their heirs. This law of tenure prevented both extreme poverty and overgrown wealth, and greatly attached the people to the country in which they had permanent homes, associated with memories of their ancestors and with the hopes of their posterity, and made them interested in preserving public order and maintaining the supremacy of the laws of the State.

On their small estates the people had to exercise frugality and industry to obtain a comfortable subsistence, and this general necessity tended to elevate the dignity of labor and give to every citizen the proud and ennobling feeling of personal independence. No system of laws upon this subject was ever devised by human wisdom so much in harmony with the general objects and purposes of the law-giver and better calculated to develop a free, enlightened, virtuous and patriotic people.

The enjoyment of civil and religious liberty seems to inspire the noblest emotions of the human heart, to expand the intellect, to give breadth and grandeur to the imagination, and is the very life-spring of genius. The brightest pages in history are those which glow with the deeds and fame of the heroes and martyrs of intellectual, civil and religious freedom. They were the great leaders of all progress in civilization, and but for the light which their spirits shed the world would still be in the darkness of ignorance, superstition and barbarism. The spirit of freedom kindled the fires of genius which have illumined the ages. It gave courage, endurance, energy and power to the heroes of Thermopylæ, Marathon and Salamis. It guided the skilful chisel of the sculptor as he wrought the matchless and immortal productions of art. It woke the highest notes of the Grecian lyre and poured the splendors of eloquence around the Acropolis of Athens and the Senate Chamber and Forum of Rome.

We will not follow the brilliant achievements of the spirit of freedom through the modern world, when, conjoined with the spirit of Christianity, they seemed to rise like a new sun from a dark moral and intellectual chaos, calling into life the slumbering energies of man, and rising slowly but surely to that zenith where it will cover the earth with the vivifying light of peace, liberty, love and holiness, even "as the waters cover the sea."

The spirit of freedom existed in a remarkable degree among the ancient Hebrews, and was greatly intensified by their religious faith and their peculiar situation among the nations. They were surrounded by the great oriental despotism, were in the direct line of ancient war, conquest and commerce; and by actual observation and experience they were acquainted with the horrors and demoralizing influences of subjugation and slavery. They were in the times of their national power and freedom a remarkably brave people, and in many of their contests the odds were greatly against them, and the preservation of their nationality and free institutions for nearly a thousand years is one of the great miracles of history. They had, during the long period of their national existence, abundant cause to believe that the Everlasting Arms were around them, and that the flaming sword of the Cherubim guarded their hallowed land; and in their fervid imaginations they could well call Jehovah their strength and shield and high tower. Great and glorious facts, and not fancies, were the sources of their love of freedom and country, and the inspirations of their sublime poetry.

This love of freedom and country—the most striking political characteristic of the Hebrews—continued during the whole of their national existence. How beautifully was it exhibited, even in captivity, when they sang in words that glowed with patriotism and glittered with tears:

"By the rivers of Babylon, there we sat down, yea, we wept when we remembered Zion.   *   *   *   *   *   *
If I forget thee, O, Jerusalem, let my right hand forget her cunning.
If I do not remember thee let my tongue cleave to the roof of my mouth, if I prefer not Jerusalem above my chief joy."

The Jews, from the time of the Babylonish captivity until finally subjugated by Roman power, never showed the humble and submissive spirits of slaves. Under Persian, Greek and Roman rule they were generally treated with more liberality and kindness than other conquered nations, and, with the exception of the oppressions of Antiochus Epiphanes, they were allowed to observe their ceremonial and national laws and customs. They were conservative in their natures, obedient to just laws, and opposed to revolutions for trivial causes. But the exercise of any despotic authority which threatened to overthrow or materially change their religious institutions, at once kindled into flame the smouldering embers of religious zeal, liberty and patriotism, and without counting odds or the consequences they rushed to arms and fought with desperate valor. No pages in human history are more brilliant with deeds of sublime endurance and heroic valor than those which record the struggles of the Maccabæan brothers for the altars and tenets of their religious faith and the land of their fathers.

In the memorable seige of Jerusalem under Titus, and in the awful finale at Masada, the Jews exhibited a burning patriotism, lofty heroism and self-devotion never equalled in terific sublimity in all the horrid tragedies of war and the overthrow of nations. The history of two centuries taught Hadrian that while their nation had an organized existence the Jews never could be made willing and submissive subjects to the despotism of the Cæsars; and he determined upon their extermination or complete dispersion. The sorrows, misfortunes and oppressions of twenty centuries have not destroyed their national characteristics. Their spirits have never been subdued to the abject condition of slavery, but they have always manifested hatred and scorn for their oppressors, and have borne the agonies of torture and the contumely of contempt with the sublime courage and endurance of martyrs. They have passed through more terrible ordeals than any other people, and they have come forth from every fiery furnace of persecution without even the smell of the flames upon the unchanged and unconsumed garments of their ancient faith. Feelings so deeply implanted and so indestructible, either by force or time, must have glowed with the grandest intensity and energy in the age of their national pride, power and glory, and kindled the highest poetic inspirations.

A spirit of national unity was a marked and distinguishing feature of the Hebrew nation. They were the chosen people of Jehovah, all the descendants of Abraham—the most venerable character in history—and were all heirs of the rich blessings and glorious hopes of that covenant which God made and so after reaffirmed to their great national fathers. They were continually reminded of this covenant by the rite of circumcision, and the dust of the earth and the sands of the seashore were emblems of their numerous posterity, and the glorious stars of heaven that every night shone above them symbolized the blessings which they were to shed over all the nations and races of coming ages. This covenant was the Magna Charta of their destiny, the vital principle of their civil and political institutions, mingled with all their history and illumined national and individual aspirations with the light of Messianic hope. In every subsequent age of their dispersion this covenant made the Holy Land the sacred home of their hearts, and sustained their sorely tried and fainting spirts as they suffered centuries of wrong, oppression, misfortune and disaster.

This spirit of national unity was also kept in fresh and vigorous life by the requirements and observances of the ceremonial law. Three times in each year they were required to go up to the Sanctuary and participate in the celebration of the great national festivals. There they witnessed the solemn and imposing rites and ceremonies of their religious worship, and were forcibly reminded of the great events and scenes which illumined the annals of their race. These three great national festivals were peculiar to them as a people and were associated with ideas of liberty, prosperity and nationality under the care of an ever-watchful providence.

The Passover was a memorial of the birthday of their freedom; the Pentecost celebrated the giving of the law, which organized them into a distinct and independent nation, and the Feast of Tabernacles reminded them of the blessings of liberty and kindly social intercourse which their forefathers enjoyed in the simple dwellings in the wilderness, which were ever beneath the light or shadow of Jehovah's presence.

The Feast of Tabernacles was the last great annual festival. It came on the fifth day after the great Day of Atonement on which the sins of Israel were removed, and covenant relations with God were restored. It was also called the Feast of Ingathering, as it came at the end of the year, when all the harvests and fruits had been gathered in. With a sense of pardoned sin and with the prospect of plenty, it was a good time to give thanks and sing. Some of the most joyous Psalms were written for this occasion and the days of this feast were the most gladsome of all the year. This feast was also regarded as typical of the greater feast which God was preparing for his people in heaven at the final harvest at the end of the world; when all the work of earth would be done; when the fruits of toil and care and obedience would all be gathered in, and all trials and sorrows and sufferings would be over in the home of everlasting joy and rest.

These festivals were celebrated with various sacrificial observances, with songs, with music and the sacred dance; and such assemblages were well calculated to keep alive their national patriotism; the fraternal relationship of the tribes, and their confidence and trust in Jehovah; and their imaginations were excited and illumined by the solemn and imposing ceremonies of the sanctuary, which were memorials of a glorious past and types of a higher and nobler destiny.

We know that the Olympic Games were strong bonds of union among the States of Greece, and had great influence in developing the courage and physical energies, and the intellect and genius of that gifted and brilliant people. Like influences and results were produced by like causes in other ancient and modern nations, but no nation has ever existed which was so thoroughly and so permanently nationalized as the Hebrews. The "Scattered Nation," and its wild, roaming kinsmen of the desert, are the only peoples who have endured the storms of centuries, as long as the pyramids.

We will now refer to the piety of the Hebrews as another powerful element in elevating their national culture. They were by far the most devout people of the ancient world, and their religious belief was the life breath of their nationality. The dream of Jacob at Bethel was a type of Hebrew spiritual life, and to their fervid fancies the mystic ladder was never withdrawn. In ardent faith they felt that hosts of angels were encamped around their dwellings and accompanied their journeyings, and sometimes they could hear divine footsteps in the murmuring groves, and they believed that on the hills and mountains were horses and chariots of fire that guarded their sacred heritage.

In all ages of the world and among all nations the idea of God has given the highest beauty and grandeur to human thought. This idea produced the splendid temples of antiquity, whose ruins still show the taste and elegance of the culture of the nations who reared them. The human mind has ever sought after God, recognizing Him as the great first cause of the life and energy that pervades the universe and fills it with harmony, beauty and beneficence. The most grand and sublime conceptions of every people are to be found in their religious belief. In the studio of the artist his grandest ideals are in some way connected with the great First Cause of symmetry and beauty.

The Gothic structures of Mediæval Europe, and the magnificent temples of more modern times, with their elevated arches and lofty spires, are representations of the aspirations of man after God. The Great Spirit of the American Indian tribes is the source of their most beautiful legends and superstitions, and of their richest language. The most barbarous nations, sunk to the lowest condition of degredation and debasement, have some noble conceptions of an unseen and powerful ruler. There seems to be an universal law of nature that prompts the human heart to seek to know something of the Infinite and to hold communion with Him in the language of poetry and prayer.

The most beautiful authologies of the Greeks are their sacred songs, which glow with intense feelings and beautiful thought. Their mythology was the principle source of their poetry and art, which have so much refined the taste and enlarged and enriched the literary treasures of the world They had divinities for everything. The thunder was the angry voice of Jupiter on high Olympus, and the lightning the flash of his terrible thunderbolts. Their mountains were the thrones and their plains and valleys the council chambers, the battlefields and the habitations of the gods In every tree some Dryad was dwelling and Nymphs were ever pouring dew drops upon the flowers. On every stream the Naiads were singing and Apollo and the tuneful Muses were waking the echoes of every hill and vale with ethereal lyres. Far out on the shining seas the Nereids were giving music to the waves. The breath of Æolus was the storm that stirred into fury the seething billows which the Halcyones, with soft and soothing melodies, lulled into gentle slumbers. Every thing that was bright, joyous, musical and beautiful in nature was the gift or was under the care of some superhuman being in some way connected with the immortals. Every household had its tutelary divinities that sanctified the hearthstone, guarded the cradle of infancy, guided the wayward footsteps of maturer years, and whispered of Elysium and the Isles of the Blessed to the aged and the dying.

The mythology of the Greeks, although in some respects so fascinating and beautiful, presented many disgusting and shameful scenes; and many of their deities were guilty of horrid crimes and enormities and the most beastly vices ever practiced by degraded man.

How completely does the sensuous polytheism of the Greeks sink into nothingness when compared with the sublime spiritual monotheism of the Hebrews. An uncreated God, as unity of infinite wisdom, power and immaculate purity and holiness, existing from everlasting to everlasting seated upon a throne in the heavens high and lifted up; clothed in garments of resplendent light, and crowned with ineffable glory and majesty; surrounded by myriads of angels and archangels, Cherubim and Seraphim, doing His will with gladness, and with faces veiled with their wings ever singing to the music of golden harps the lofty songs of eternal praise. With omniscient eye He read all the secrets of the present and the past and contemplated the coming events of the future; to Him even ages were not moments of time, and eternity but an unending now. He was also regarded as Omnipresent and Omnipotent, not only dwelling in the heavens, but everwhere present and controlling every part of the illimitable universe and all created things, not as a pantheistic, animating and commingling element, but as a separate, independent, Supreme Creator and Governor. He spoke worlds into being by a word or the exercise of omnific will. He measured the waters in the hollow of His hand, meted out the heavens with the span, comprehended the dust of the earth in a measure, weighed the mountains in scales and the hills in a balance. He shook the earth on her deep foundations so that the pillars thereof trembled, and "He toucheth the hills and they smoke." He guided the heavenly hosts in their unerring orbits. "He telleth the number of the stars. He calleth them all by their names." And yet amidst the grandest displays of His wisdom and power, He manifested His holiness, truth justice and benevolence; and while He would "by no means clear the guilty," He was "merciful and gracious, long suffering and abundant in goodness and truth."

With the providential care of an All-Wise Father He watched and blessed the humblest creatures and works of His hand. "They all wait upon Him and He giveth them their meat in due season." He sendeth the springs into the valleys which ran among the hills and gave drink to the beasts of the field to quench their thirst. "He watereth the hills from His chambers," and freshens the verdure of the pastures for the cattle. He giveth habitations to the birds, and teacheth them to build their nests and sing among the branches. He filleth the trees with sap and maketh them rejoice and clap their hands. He made a home for the leviathan in the deep, wide sea that he might play among the waters. He distilled the sparkling dew and perfumed the breath of the morning. He clothed the flowers with exquisite beauty. "He giveth snow like wool; He scattereth the hoar frost like ashes." He fed the young ravens when they cried. "He made the high hills a refuge for the wild goats and the rocks for the conies." With what astonished and rapturous admiration did the Psalmist sing, "Yea, the sparrow hath found an house, and the swallow a nest for herself, where she may lay her young; even Thine altars, O, Lord of Hosts, my King and my God."

Without making full verbal quotations I have stated a few of the numerous ideas and expressions of the Hebrew bards as they looked forth upon the glories of nature. They did not observe the works of creation as natural philosophers, but contemplated them with the fervent and loving admiration of the soul. They regarded all the objects of nature as their kindred under the care of the same universal Father who with tender and beneficent love provided daily for the wants and welfare of his great family. Their poetry of nature appeals to the heart and understanding, as they combine beauty with truth and animate both with intense sympathetic feelings.

The sublime and devout religious faith of the Hebrews was elevated and strengthened by the continual manifestations of Jehovah's presence. If they went astray He scourged them back to duty, and when they were obedient subjects, their corn and wine increased and their land was blessed with peace and abounded with plenty. To them the Tabernacle was Jehovah's earthly dwelling place and the magnificent Temple of Solomon made Jerusalem "The City of the Great King."

The great and controlling influence of metropolitan cities can be distinctly traced in the history of all civilized nations. In them are concentrated the industry, wealth and the intellectual, moral and political energies of the people, and are thus concentrated central forces that generate and regulate peculiar systems of civilization. This fact is so well established that I need not refer to the numerous instances presented in history.

In the time of David Jerusalem was made the political and religious metropolis of the Hebrew State and became endeared to the people by many proud and patriotic associations, and was consecrated by the hallowed services and emblems of their religious worship. Their love for their Holy City was dearer, deeper and stronger than their love of life, and this love has endured through the long line of their descendants for nearly thirty centuries. Even now the few dejected and persecuted Jews who dwell in or visit Jerusalem, every week gather around the few broken and defaced stones of their ruined temple and pour forth wailing words and bitter tears, and with a sublime and unshaken faith long for the building of the walls of Zion. An all-absorbing and enduring love like this is itself an epic of wondrous beauty, pathos and sublimity.

With their language, with their history, with their beautiful country, with their sublime and imposing religious faith, and with their Holy City and fatherland, can it be a matter of surprise that the Hebrew bards produced the grandest and richest poetry ever read by man ?

LECTURE IX.

ART CULTURE. THE TABERNACLE AND TEMPLE.
THE PASSOVER.

In observing the influence which poetry has exerted upon the intellectual progress and æsthetic culture of other nations, we are naturally led to inquire why the Hebrews did not make higher advancement in the fine arts which are kindred to, and usually associated with the art of poetry, in which they attained such surpassing excellence. We will now proceed to examine briefly this interesting subject.

The history of human progress shows that poetry is the only one of the fine arts that ever attained any high degree of excellence among a primitive people. It has, however, nearly always preceded and created that æsthetic culture which, in a more advanced stage of civilization, has given rise to the kindred arts of elegant architecture, music, painting and sculpture.

Egypt is generally regarded as the cradle of the arts and sciences, but that people never produced any poetry of the highest order, and never became eminent in the fine arts. Their architecture was grand, massive and imposing, and their painting and sculpture were stiff, inelegant, and greatly wanting in the elements of beauty. They taught the Greeks the first lessons of art, which that refined and imaginative people carried to a degree of excellence which has been the delight and admiration of all succeeding ages.

The refined and elegant culture of the Greeks may in a great degree be attributed to the poems of Homer. These sublime poems were produced in a fabulous and heroic age and remained for more than three centuries an almost unwritten minstrelsy which lived with vivid freshness and power in the hearts of the semi-civilized Greeks, inspiring and preparing them for their glorious intellectual and political destiny. When these poems were collected, arranged and reduced to writing by the accomplished Pisistratus they constituted the principal literature of the nation, and were read and studied in the schools of Athens and the cities of Ionia. It is said in fable that Cadmus sowed the teeth of a dragon and thus produced the stalwart warriors of Thebes. It may be said in metaphor that Homer sowed the prolific germs of imaginative thought which sprang up into an abundant harvest that has enriched the world with the productions of poetry and art.

During the period of the Roman republic there was but little poetic literature, and we find the people brave, intellectual and practical, founding wise civil institutions and beneficent laws; building splendid aqueducts, paved roads and massive structures for the purposes of war and commerce, but they made little advancement in æsthetic culture.

The poetry and cultivated taste of the conquered Greeks planted germs in Italy which sprang up in luxuriant fruitage, and soon the republican city of brick became the imperial city of marble, and the whole land was filled with elegant villas, temples and palaces, which were crowded and adorned with the highest achievements of artistic genius.

The dawn that followed the midnight of the Middle Ages was beautified by the roseate light of poetry. In my first lecture I referred at some length to the influence of poetry in forming national tastes and in producing the high development of the kindred arts of architecture, music, painting and sculpture. This influence of poetry seems to constitute a primary and fundamental law of refined civilization. To this general law the history of the Hebrews furnishes a singular exception. They were a highly poetical people, and made some advancement in architecture, music and many of the useful arts, but they made little progress in painting and sculpture. At an early period they became familiar with Egyptian art, but they did not develop it into elegance and beauty like the Greeks, who in a subsequent age received information from the same great primal source of civilization. We propose to inquire briefly into some of the reasons why the Hebrews in this department of refined culture did not accomplish as much as the Greeks. In mental and physical organization the Hebrews were not inferior to the Greeks, and both races were remarkable for personal beauty and graceful symmetry of bodily development. The Greek artists in the young athletæ of the gymnasium had appropriate models to guide their ideal conceptions of divinities and the demigods of the heroic ages. They were always surrounded with matchless forms of female beauty and grace. Greece, Ionia and the Ægean Isles presented numberless scenes of picturesque loveliness.

The Hebrew artists might have found many an Asahel as light of foot as the wild roe, and many an Absalom the perfection of manly beauty. The achievements of the fabled Hercules were not superior to those of the Nazarite Judge who rent the young lion and who so easily bore away the ponderous gates of Gaza, and overwhelmed in terrific ruin the crowded temple of Dagon. The daughters of Zion, as they glided through the mingling mazes of the dance to the sound of timbrels and harps, might well have kindled the inspirations of genius longing for ideals of the graceful and the beautiful. The Hebrews were the highest type of the Shemitic races, and the Greeks were the noblest of the children of Japheth, and both were highly imaginative and loved the beautiful in nature, which they found in such rich profusion in the heaven-blest lands which they inhabited, and both expressed their ardent admiration of the glories of nature in the finest strains of poetry. It was not the lack of taste and genius, or the want of suitable subjects, or poverty of materials, that prevented the Hebrews from attaining superior excellence in imitative art, for their history and poetry have been the rich fields from which modern genius has gleaned its most splendid conceptions and models for painting and sculpture.

The principle cause of difference between the Hebrews and the Greeks in artistic development was the diversity of their religious faith. In every age among pagan nations there has been a strong feeling in the human heart that prompted man to seek for some object of sensuous worship. The Greeks had no divine revelation to guide them, and their ardent fancies created, or highly embellished the objects of their adoration. They were deeply impressed by natural beauty, which they supposed was produced and preserved by supernatural and ethereal beings. These were the *beau ideals* of their religious aspirations and their plastic genius gave them tangible and visible existence in painting and sculpture. We find that the highest efforts of genius in the fine arts represented religious feeling and sentiment. The mythology of the Greeks was the rich and prolific source of their art inspiration. The spirit of Mediæval Christianity was displayed in Gothic cathedrals and minsters, and in a later and more enlightened age kindled the genius of the Old Masters, who filled the cities of Europe with the noblest miracles of art.

The Hebrews had but one place of public worship, and both the Tabernacle and Temple were built under instructions from Jehovah and were sanctified by the mysterious symbols of His presence. Thus their genius for sacred architecture, painting and sculpture was not called into exercise, enlarged and refined by the frequent construction of gorgeous temples. They had none of the incentives and opportunities which stimulated and cultivated the genius of the artists of Greece, Rome and Modern Europe. The Temple that stood in the midst of their holy city was built by Tyrian architects, and was more magnificent in architectural splendor and beauty than any structure ever reared by genius, but to them it was too sacred to be imitated, it was the dwelling place of the Most High. Their religious truths and principles were marked out and defined in the heaven-directed laws and institutions of Moses with precision and exactitude, and were too solemn and impressive for the creations of fancy. The voice of Jehovah proclaimed in tones of thunder from the lurid cloud-temple of Sinai, "Thou shalt not make unto thee any graven image, or any likeness of anything that is in heaven above, or that is in the earth beneath; or that is in the water under the earth." They had heard the awful penalties denounced against the violations of this law, and often witnessed dread judgments on the disobedient. They were continually surrounded and overshadowed by religious ceremonials, grandly gorgeous and imposing, and their ideas of Jehovah Sabaoth were invested with a sublimity of awe too exalted for art, and could only be fitly expressed in the language of divine inspiration which elevated and enraptured the soul. In the times of their highest religious purity they could not imagine a sensuous representation of the attributes of Deity; omnipotence, omnipresence, infinity and the perfection of holiness, surrounded by that ineffable light and glory before which even the angels veiled their faces with their shining wings.

When the Hebrews, under the demoralizing influences which surrounded them, departed from the observances of the ceremonial law and neglected their high spiritual worship, we find them following the examples of pagan nations and setting up images of sensuous and idolatrous adoration, but they were always brought back to their sacred allegiance by various corrective providences.

We will mention only one other cause for the inferiority

of the Hebrews in the fine arts. The history of these arts shows that they have never attained a high degree of excellence, except in a commercial and luxurious nation, where many individuals had accumulated large fortunes and had abundant leisure and a cultivated taste for refined enjoyments. The civil and political institutions of the Hebrews were designed for an agricultural and not a commercial people. They were all descended from the same common ancestor, and under their free institutions were entitled to equal social, civil and political privileges. There were no proud and imperious nobles and princes claiming a more distinguished lineage and higher prerogatives than their fellow citizens, and who were desirous of perpetuating and rendering more impressive their social position, fame and power by costly palaces adorned with the rich and elaborate elegancies of art. There was no aristocracy of wealth who expended accumulated treasures in the profuse extravagances of pomp and pride. There were no large communities of slaves to rear massive and ostentatious structures like the pyramids, temples and treasure cities of Egypt, and the gorgeous palaces and hanging gardens of Babylon to perpetuate the fame of cruel and licentious despots. The laws and institutions of Moses—to which we have already referred—prevented the accumulation of large individual fortunes.

In Palestine there were no great cities and commercial emporiums, the seats of voluptuous ease and luxurious refinements. The great mass of the people dwelt in villages and hamlets, and were forced by necessity to spend their time in watching their flocks and herds, and in cultivating their small patrimonial estates. Thus they remained a rural and pastoral people, living apart from other nations and retaining even to the time of the Babylonish captivity the simple manners and customs of their patriarchal ancestors.

I will now briefly refer to the elevating and refining

influences produced upon Hebrew taste and culture by their sacred architecture, music and the splendid rites employed in the ceremonial services of the sanctuary. The Tabernacle erected in the wilderness by the heaven-inspired genius of Moses, Bazaleel and Aholiab, was a gorgeous pavillion gleaming with silver and gold and with the brightest coloring; and the inner curtains were richly embroidered with Cherubim and other beautiful figures of delicate and elaborate workmanship and joined to each other with finely chased clasps of gold. There was an awful sanctity in the silence and solitude of the Holy of Holies. No one ever went behind its mysterious separating veil except the High Priest, and he but once a year, after being sanctified by the most solemn and elaborate purifications. In it were placed the golden Ark of the Covenant containing the tables of the law, the pot of manna and Aaron's wonder-working rod, and above the Mercy Seat stood with overshadowing wings the guardian golden Cherubim. No light of day entered this sacred and silent penetralia, but it was always illumined by the radiant glory of the Shechinah, the symbol of Jehovah's presence. During the desert pilgrimage the Tabernacle was always pitched in the centre of the encamping tribes, and above it stood in silent grandeur the pillar of cloud or the pillar of fire, which was the visible leader of the marching hosts. When the cloud moved from its resting place, the silver trumpets of the priests were sounded and the clear notes rang out in soul-stirring music over the white tents of Israel, and echoed and re-echoed among the valleys, hills and grand mountains of the desert. When Israel reached the Promised Land and found permanent homes among its green mountains, vine-clad hills and fertile valleys, and ceased from warfare and wandering, their love and veneration for the Tabernacle were greatly increased, as it had become the political and religious centre of the nation, and three times in each year the kindred tribes assembled in its sacred courts to join in its hallowed services. When they had returned to their homes from the great national festivals their memories of the Tabernacle were always fresh and vivid, as they knew that twice each day, as the sun arose over the Syrian desert, and as it sank into the waves of the great sea, the silver trumpets sounded, the sacrificial fires blazed on the brazen altar and the cloud of incense ascended from the golden altar in the Holy Place, as an atonement for their sins and an invocation of the continued blessings of Jehovah.

Everything connected with the Hebrew ritual was impressive and splendid. There was the High Priest clothed in the bright colored ephod, clasped in front by the breastplate which was sanctified by the Urim and Thummim, and sparkled with precious symbolic jewels, and on his brow a shining coronet of gold proclaimed him "Holy to the Lord." Around him were the priests, arrayed in rich sacerdotal vestures, preparing the offerings for the sacrifice. On both sides of the brazen altar stood immense choirs of white robed Levites pouring forth in antiphonal strains the sacred songs of praise and thanksgiving, accompanied with rich notes of instrumental music, together forming grand waves of melody, which made the heavens and hills resound with responsive echoing raptures. The Tabernacle worship was continued for more than four hundred years, and these religious ceremonies were made still more splendid and imposing in the temple service.

I will not attempt to describe, at any length, the temple which Solomon built unto the God of Israel, and embellished with the riches of exhaustless treasures and all the glories of Tyrian art. The sanctuary of the temple was built of smoothly hewed stones, adjusted to each other with the nicest precision. It was covered within and without with cedar boards richly carved with Cherubim, palm trees and open flowers, overlaid with pure gold.

The inner walls and ceiling were also garnished with precious stones, and the floor was a shining pavement of gold. The ten golden tables were laden with golden vessels encrusted with jewels, and the ten golden candlesticks, from their numerous lamps fed with fragrant oil, sent forth a continuous breath of perfume and a blaze of light that filled the whole apartment with coruscating splendors. The sanctuary was surrounded with stories of chambers, with porticoes and galleries, and with massive walls and towers of the whitest marble. The whole temple structure, with its costly and precious decorations and adornments, rested upon the top of the sacred mountain, and on a clear day it glowed and gleamed and glittered in radiant glory like a magnificent palace of the sun "From diamond quarries hewn and rocks of gold." It was hallowed by the symbols of Jehovah's presence, and His voice of benediction had resounded through its sanctuaries. Well might the heart of a pious and patriotic Hebrew have swelled with the noblest sentiments and feelings as he beheld this pride of his country and the glorious temple of his God; while all the emotions of his soul bursted forth in rapturous song.

We will now consider, with more minuteness of detail than we have heretofore done, some of the scenes presented in the celebration of the Passover. We select this one of the great national festivals of the Hebrews, as important events in their later history have rendered it so memorable and interesting to the Christian world.

In the spring time of every year the families of Israel commenced their annual pilgrimage to the holy city, and from the mountains of Lebanon, the hills of Kedar, the plains of Syria, the shores of the great sea, and from all the green valleys of the holy land, in gathering caravans went up to Jerusalem to worship, singing songs of joy and praise and carrying offerings for the Temple. To them it was a sacred pilgrimage, rendered joyous by the association of old friends, and every resting place was a familiar spot surrounded by the beauties of nature and hallowed by pleasant memories. Everywhere along the journey they witnessed scenes renowned in heroic and sacred story, and heard names made musical by the melody of song. And when from the mountains round about Jerusalem they saw their sacred temple and holy city gleaming with the reflected glories of the sunlight, with feelings of intense devotion they sang a sublime liturgical Psalm in choral joy and melody that seemed to make even the trees of the wood to rejoice and the green hills shout with gladness. In the hospitable homes of the city they found a cordial welcome, and everywhere in house and tent and booth families gathered at the table of the paschal supper and in effectionate and holy communion celebrated the great national feast. They were not wearied from journeying but spent the night in talking over the memorable events in their nation's history, and with grateful hearts returned thanks to Jehovah for His manifold beneficences. They eagerly longed for the coming morning when the great congregation would enter the gates of the Lord's house with thanksgiving and praise.

I will now attempt to describe briefly a scene which might have been witnessed by a pious Hebrew from the top of Mount Olivet on the first day of the Passover. The kindling rays of the dawn have tipped with silvery brightness the summits of the dark mountains of Moab and the gray twilight is gliding silently and softly over the awakening city and amid the gloaming of the wide extended landscape. All things in nature have waked from the solemn stillness and slumbers of the night, and with fresh, glad voices seem to hail the coming light, while soft mystic melodies are floating on the ambient air. Now he sees more distinctly the white tents on the mountain sides and in the deep valleys and can hear the noise of eager footsteps and the busy hum of voices that tell him that the devout hosts of Israel are preparing for the morning sacrifice. In the East are slowly spreading the gorgeous curtains of the earthly tabernacle, gleaming in purple and gold and glorious in beauty, resting on mountain pillars, and covering flowery plains, verdant hills and fruitful valleys. And now the sun—nature's high priest—enters through the beautiful gates of the morning and with grand majestic march moves up his celestial pathway and with bountiful beneficence fills the earthly tabernacle with golden radiance, blessedness and joy; and nature worships its Great Creator and sends up anthems of thanksgiving and the richest incense to His holy temple not made with hands, eternal in the heavens. Now man begins his worship, and the silver trumpets from the temple wake the echoes that slumbered among the mountains of Zion, and clear and musical the notes come over the the gliding Kidron and are ringing among the cedars, the figtrees, the clustering vines and waving palms of Olivet.

It is the hour of the morning sacrifice and the mingled clouds from the altars of incense and burnt offering are rising above the gleaming pinnacles, the stately porches and beautiful gates of the Temple, and are spreading like Jehovah's protecting wing over the assembled people and the hallowed land. From every house in Jerusalem, and from the tents of Israel, rejoicing worshipers are crowding up the marble steps of the temple courts and with voices and emotions gushing from grateful hearts are joining the glorious harmonies of the temple choirs as with exultant joy they sing the sublime morning anthem. The grand and imposing scenes which accompanied the celebration of the great national festivals must have made a profound and ineffaceable impression upon the pious, patriotic and imaginative Hebrew, as he earnestly believed that they but dimly prefigured the Messianic glories that were to beam with supernatural splendors around the mountains of Zion and make Jerusalem the joy of the whole earth.

LECTURE X.

THE AGES OF DAVID AND SOLOMON. THE INFLUENCE OF HEBREW POETRY UPON CHRISTIAN HYMNOLOGY.

The age of David and Solomon is generally regarded as the zenith period of the national prosperity, power and literary glory of the Hebrews. The reigns of these two princes, in some respects, present a striking contrast, and yet both contributed greatly to social and intellectual progress and national development. David was the greatest king of Israel. He conquered all their enemies and extended his dominions from the borders of Egypt to the Euphrates, and his turbulent reign was illumined with the splendors of civic and military achievements.

Solomon was a peaceful prince, more munificent in his bounties and more successful in promoting national prosperity and advancement than the brilliant Pericles or the wise and pacific Augustus. He built the Temple, the most rich and gorgeous structure ever erected by the hands of men, and he beautified Jerusalem with public works and palaces and made it the home of industry, science and the useful arts, and the centre of a rich and refined social and intellectual culture which attracted the wonder and admiration of other nations. He sent the messengers of commerce to bring wealth, comfort and luxuries from distant shores and the "Isles of the Gentiles." He exhibited the talent and skill of human diplomacy by establishing friendly relations with neighboring kingdoms, and his justice and wisdom made him an arbiter of nations, and induced thousands of strangers to make their homes in a land blessed with his enlightened laws and beneficent institutions. He reared cities in the wilderness, laid out highways and planted gardens in the desert, and gave his people the blessings of peace. These two reigns continued for more than fifty years, and a period so brilliant with the triumphs of war and the glories of peace must have greatly stimulated and elevated the genius of a people who were constantly expecting and earnestly longing for a golden age of national greatness and splendor, when the promised Messiah, as a magnificent prince, would establish his ever-enduring throne upon Mount Zion and make Jerusalem the metropolitan city of all nations. Such intense hopes and vivid fancies were well calculated to call forth the loftiest efforts of poetic genius.

We may well believe that David and Solomon were representative men of their nation, and that their sublime productions which have come down to us present but few of the many thoughts and emotions that gushed from the glowing hearts and minds of their countrymen in the richest language and clothed with imagery as multiform as that which nature furnishes in her glorious gallery of the earth, sea and skies.

We believe that a poet is the creature of his age, and in a great degree collects and reflects the spirit of his people. The circumstances and influences by which he is surrounded are the inspirations of his genius. He concentrates these various intellectual, moral and natural influences and gives them new forms of life, power and beauty, just as the lens of science collects and concentrates the diffused rays of light into a more brilliant and burning glow. The poetic feelings of the Hebrew people, produced by the causes to which we have referred, were the natural influences which kindled the genius of David when an humble shepherd boy, tending his fathers flocks in the quiet valleys of Bethlehem, he tuned his simple harp to immortal melodies; and his songs were elevated to sublimer strains when he experienced the merciful providences of God, shielding him from the relentless persecutions of Saul and guiding his pathway through the vicissitudes and dangers of his stormy life. Solomon was the child of the much loved Bathsheba, and received the constant care, instruction and fervent affections of his noble and highly gifted father. He was surrounded by the taste and elegance of court life, and his youthful genius was heightened and brightened by the gorgeous ceremonies and glorious minstrelsy and music of the tabernacle service which David had so admirably regulated. In this connection we only speak of the natural gifts, advantages and attainments of David and Solomon. They were also prophets and inspired poets, and in their writings, preserved in the Old Testament, they were under the guidance of the Holy Spirit.

The writings of the prophets who preceded the Captivity are highly poetical and furnish strong evidence of the imaginative temperament of their people. Rebellion, disunion and the bitterness of sectional and political hatred had destroyed the unity of national life and broken down many of the strong bulwarks which had so long preserved the chosen people from the demoralizing influences of the surrounding nations, and they had almost forgotten the God and the sacred institutions of their fathers. At this period of degeneracy the prophets were sent as divine messengers to warn, instruct and guide the people, and they knew full well that they could not arrest the tides of rapid decline in any other manner than by appealing in impassioned and glowing eloquence to the intense and fervid natures of their countrymen. The prophecies are grand national poems of varied styles and harmonies. At one time they are illumined with bright pictures of the events of the past and the glorious hopes of the future; then in weeping and pleading melodies they speak to the finest and most tender feelings of the heart; and then they utter strong denunciations against sin, error and disobedience, and then kindle and burn with indignant and eloquent imprecations against the nations who had oppressed and corrupted Israel. We will reserve the subject of the prophecies for more extended consideration in a future lecture.

We will now take a rapid glance at the influences exerted by Hebrew poetry upon the literatures and civilization of subsequent ages. We have already spoken of the influence of some of the great poems of classic antiquity upon the æsthetic culture of mankind. They were crystalized and made immortal by the power of human genius, but they have operated upon only a comparatively small class of educated men, and their influences have not permeated the great mass of the people of subsequent times and aroused their noblest emotions and awakened their moral perceptions and intellectual energies. Many of the Hebrew bards lived centuries before Homer and their great poems are now read, even at this distant age, with the highest pleasure and profit by millions who know nothing of poetry as a fine art and whose tastes have never been cultivated by the elegancies of classic learning. These poems gave an unyielding national cohesiveness to the Jewe during the post-exillian period of their history when the conquests of Alexander, the desolating wars of his successors, and the all-grasping ambition of Rome were continually changing the boundaries and destinies of States, and making human society a vast boiling and bloody caldron of strife and revolution.

The Septuagint version of these poems, through the medium of the elegant and cultivated language of Greece, transfused their influence into ancient learning and civilization, and thus prepared the world for those glorious realities which they had dimly but grandly prefigured. They became blended with the teachings and beauties of the New Dispensation with as natural and harmonious an affinity as the rudy and glowing light of the morning dawn melts into the effulgence of the rising sun.

It is not my purpose in these lectures to refer even in a

cursory manner to the New Testament, for I would not by a hasty sketch do injustice to such a rich and extensive subject. I will say, however, that it contains numerous passages and scenes of exquisite beauty and tender pathos. The Sermon on the Mount is not only the most perfect discourse ever uttered, but it is a poem of incomparable beauty, glowing with the light of divine love, and the Beatitudes must have some of the heavenly sweetness of the songs which the angels sing. The speeches and writings of Saint Paul in richness of thought, in terseness, force and elegance of diction are equal to the best productions of Athenian genius; and the sublime visions of the Apocalypse were painted with the brightest pencil of poetic prophecy. The New Testament develops the spiritual beauties of Hebrew literature, just as the sunshine causes the diamond to gleam with a brilliancy of lustre that was not visible in the dimness of the twilight.

The influence of Hebrew poetry upon the hymnology of the Christian Church can be distinctly traced from the earliest times. The hymn which Christ and his Apostles sang at the close of the first Lord's Supper was a psalm which had long been used in the celebration of the Passover; and from that hour on through the ages psalms and hymns and sacred songs have thrilled the heart of the Christian world, and many of their highest and richest notes of praise were those that once sounded to melody wakened on the strings of the old Hebrew lyre. During the Apostolic age and for more than a century afterwards no other songs were used in public or private devotions than

"Those strains that once did sweet in Zion glide,"

and in the churches they were sung in the antiphonal style used by Asaph and his choirs of Levites as in lofty melody they responded from each side of the brazen altar of the Temple.

In after ages there was a long and eventful struggle between the refined and elegant mythology, philosophy and poetry of paganism and the simple rites and doctrines, and the sublime literature of Christianity for supremacy in the Roman empire. Those were indeed times that tried men's souls, and they exhibited a lofty courage and sublime fortitude that have no parallels in the annals of human heroism. As the primitive church passed through the terrible ordeal of the martyr ages the courage and endurance of Christian heroes were elevated and ennobled by memories of Israel's trials and triumphs and sustained by a living faith in the same Almighty Being that guarded the prophet with the horses and chariots of fire, that stopped the mouths of lions, and walked with His suffering and persecuted children through the fierce furnace fires of Babylon. Although the Church was triumphant over the principalities and powers of paganism, the brightness of its celestial armor was tarnished, it received many scars in the conflict, and departed far from the purity of its first love. Temporal success and power brought pride, wealth and worldly ambition to the descendants of the saintly fathers and heroic martyrs, and caused them to depart from the simple rites and doctrines of patristic times. But as the Church moved on its troublous pathway through the revolutions of states and empires into the thickening gloom of the Middle Ages the old Hebrew Psalter rang out, like the notes of the silver trumpets of the priests, leading and cheering the hosts of Israel in their desert journey, and its grand hymns of praise modulated to new metres swelled on the notes of Cecilian organs through the dim aisles and lofty arches of Gothic cathedrals and minsters, inspiring thousands of earnest and pious hearts with high and rapt devotion.

The mighty social, political and religious revolutions caused by the Reformation engendered strong feelings of prejudice and hatred against the Church of Rome, and some of the Reformers, uninfluenced by the example and teachings of Luther, regarded as abominations even the innocent beauties of its ceremonial service, and its elegant music and many of its sublime hymns and anthems were considered as the pagan and unholy attendants of an impure and idolatrous worship. Such feelings were manifested in a high degree by the Puritans and made them hostile even to the beautiful and spiritual liturgy of the Reformed Church of England. The bold, stern and fanatical spirit of Puritanism came over the English Protestant Church like a storm-cloud which often comes over the face of nature when fierce with the thunder and glittering with the lightning, fructifying the earth with fertilizing rains, but hiding the joyous sunlight and hushing the sweet, soft voices that breathe their melodies in God's grand earthly temple. As the storm accomplishes important and beneficent results in the economy of nature and is followed by a purer atmosphere, richer vegetation and a brighter day, so the moral and religious storm of Puritanism, although it, for a time, obscured the advancing light of progress, yet with the red rain of the blood of patriots and martyrs it fertilized the dwarfed and feeble plants of intellectual and religious freedom and caused them to spring up into more healthful and vigorous life and bear fruits and leaves for the enjoyment and healing of the nations. As the morning light with freshness and beauty follows the darkness of night, as the rainbow gleams upon the bosom of the storm, so God is ever bringing light, beauty and hope out of the confused councils of men and the revolutions of nations. The lofty enthusiasm, passionate purpose and intense religious zeal of Puritanism, darkened the earnest minds and hearts of the Puritan Fathers with bigotry and intolerance, yet it gave birth to a purer and more spiritual Christianity and produced the grandest prose and poetic literature in our language. What Christian can, without emotions of gratitude and admiration, read the eloquent productions of the old Puritan divines, so rich in thought and language and so illumined with spiritual truth. The Paradise Lost will ever stand pre-eminently glorious in English literature; and tear drops from the eyes of youth, manhood and age have fallen and will ever fall upon those immortal pages on which the Puritan Bunyan in his prison cloister traced with vivid imagery and tender pathos the dangers, difficulties, trials and triumphs of the Christian pilgrimage. In that age another poet sprang up in the bosom of the Puritan Church, whose exquisite genius glowed with the blended inspiration of the Bards of Israel and the sublime teachings of the Gospel, and he touched his hallowed harp with lyric raptures. Isaac Watts is the well recognized leader of the modern noble choir of Christian minstrels whose sacred songs, glowing with the spirit of the psalmists, prophets and apostles, will ever thrill through the church on earth, waking higher and gladder strains of melody until they blend with the seraphic harmonies of the Church in glory.

We have now concluded our hasty and imperfect enumeration of some of the causes and influences which operated most powerfully upon the Hebrews in producing their sublime and matchless poetry. In our succeeding lectures we will speak more in detail of these productions which contain so many gems of thought radiant in truth and beauty, and of inestimable value to the literature of the world.

Before concluding this lecture we deem it appropriate briefly to allude to a prevalent error and prejudice which long prevented "Bible Poetry" from exerting its full and beneficent influence upon the æsthetic culture of mankind. Since the days of the Reformation, but especially since the times of Puritanism, there have been many earnest and devout Christians who have regarded the expression "Bible Poetry" as profane and blasphemous. In their intense religious zeal they associated poetry with fiction, fable and worldly pleasures and delights.

They regarded the Bible as too sacred and truthful to be placed in profane association with the creations of human fancy. They would not admit that the Bible contained any poetry. They objected to all the modern improvements in sacred music, and could not listen with proper composure to many of the sweet and beautiful hymns of our Christian bards, which were inspired by faith and adorned with the beauty of holiness. This prejudice may exist to some extent in this country at the present day, but it is rapidly passing away before the enlightenment of our civilization and the influence of a pure and spiritual Christianity, and nearly all men of education, fine susceptibilities and cultivated tastes, now regard the Bible as not only the inspired word of God, but also as a great literary treasure and the repository of the sweetest and sublimest poetry.

Nearly every one can feel the influence of poetry, but it is almost impossible to define the meaning of the word. The definitions contained in dictionaries by no means embrace the entire signification of the term. Poetry is derived from a Greek verb, meaning *to create*, and comprehends within the scope of the ideas conveyed by the word anything in nature or art that creates, arouses or suggests elevated, pleasing or pathetic emotions and thoughts. Thus we hear and feel the poetry of music when some skillful hand wakes the witchery of the tuneful harp, or blends into harmony the low, soft, solemn and breathing melodies of the church organ. The Greeks were accustomed to associate poetry and music, and in their mythology these twin sisters of melody were believed to be under the control of the same divinities; and poets were always represented as masters of the lyre. We can well believe that the expression "prose poetry" is not a verbal paradox when we read many of the rich rhythmic and brilliant pages of history, philosophy, eloquence, criticism and science, and feel our hearts thrill with the sweetest and noblest emotions as we catch some of the spirit and musical cadences of the great word and thought painters who have illumined our prose literature with the true Promethean fire of genius.

We often hear of the "poetry of nature," and every one who is susceptible to impressions of the grand, sublime and beautiful scenes in nature, everywhere so profusely displayed, regards the expression as accurate and appropriate. Indeed nature is the true source of poetry, and any composition which is not in accordance with her principles and laws will not command lasting admiration, although the language may be glowing and rhythmical. In classic metaphor nature is called the Parnassus of poetry, and she has numerous fountains of inspiration which gush with perennial waters, of which the poet who drinks deeply becomes immortal.

We feel that it is not irreverent to speak of the "poetry of religion." Aspirations after holiness, heaven and God fill the heart with sweet emotions and the mind with lofty thoughts which ever struggle to express themselves in prayer or the joyous voice of song. The feelings of David when he wrote "As the heart panteth after the water brooks so panteth my soul after Thee, O, God," was the keynote of his rapturous and glorious minstrelsy. These earnest religious aspirations not only tuned the harps of Psalmists, Prophets and Christian minstrels, but they have filled millions of human hearts with melody and poetry which were never uttered or written in song or poem, but were breathed in silent ascriptions of thanksgiving and praise, which were heard in heaven and sounded on the rejoicing harps of the angels. Poetry, in a general sense, is the spirit of the true, the beautiful, the good, the sublime and the holy. In a more confined and technical sense it is the expression of that spirit by means of metrical and musical language. We will not endeavor to give a more accurate and comprehensive definition. We might as well attempt to hold the winds in the hollow of our hands, or imprison the sunlight that in glittering freedom sports over the landscape. Poetry is a kind of *anima mundi* that pervades the universe and produces a sublime and beautiful harmony in the natural creation, and between the ideal and the real.

God has revealed Himself to man both in His works and in His word. If in the wide domain of nature—man's earthly and temporary dwelling—the revelations of God in His works are to our natural senses so full of richness, elegance, beauty, sublimity and magnificence; so complete in order, symmetry and harmony, and so vocal with melodies, can we be surprised that the revelations which He has made in His word to our spiritual perceptions and our moral natures, which are in His image, should be radiant and musical with some of the celestial light, melody and glory of the eternal home.

A true test of the excellency of poetry is the influence which it exerts upon mankind. It is said that a well tuned harp-string untouched by mortal finger will vibrate in harmony to accordant notes made on another musical instrument. Thus poetic feeling may lie deep and silent in the heart but it utters its sweetest voice when awakened by some strain struck in unison on the lyre by the skilful hand of genius. This is the mystic power of Hebrew poetry. It is in unison with the finest and purest emotions of the human heart and will awake in the soul responsive harmonies.

Our intellectual faculties and cultivated tastes may be charmed with the musical flow and sublime imagery of Bible poetry, but we cannot realize its purest beauties, its sweetest harmonies, and its most tender pathos unless we are inspired with a faith that makes us hear the whisperings of the Holy Spirit, even as the Hebrew bards heard the voice of God in the rapt moments of inspiration.

LECTURE XI.

The Pentateuch. The Books of Ruth, Esther and Job.

A traveler of culture and imagination as he stands amidst the ruins of Egyptian Thebes and surveys the majestic memorials that rest upon the grave of a dead empire is deeply impressed with the solemn gradeur of the scene.

The brilliant light of that cloudless clime gleams upon the wrecks and relics of time, the wondrous Nile moves its volume of waters through its fertile valley from the mountains to the sea, and the tall regal palms as they wave their plumed heads to the breezes, all present scenes of life and beauty; but still the beholder feels that he is surrounded by the gloomy shadows of death. He is impressed with a solemn presence—the adumbration of a mightier power than time—which has been working the grand changes and revolutions of human destiny. Around him on every side are the evidences of a once wealthy, enlightened and powerful people, but no historic voice tells him of the times when were reared those once splendid shrines of devotion and costly palaces of ambition and pride. There are records written on the monuments and tombs of the buried race, but they are as yet almost as voiceless to mankind as the sphinx of the desert. Imagination, with eager restlessness soars into the darkness and mysteries of the regions of the silent past but brings back no light upon its wings. Much of the history of Old Egypt is covered with the deluge of oblivion, which is more impenetrable to human efforts than the chilled waters and icy ramparts that surround and guard the poles.

There is an antiquity more remote than that of Old Egypt, and it has a history that is radiant with holy and living light that speaks with eloquent voices to the human heart. throws open an invaluable treasury of truth, and spreads out fields of richness and enchanting beauty for instructive, speculative and poetic thought.

The preservation of the Scriptures of the Old Testament is indeed a wondrous miracle. They have not only survived the wrecks and ruins of time, but they have passed unharmed through the fierce furnace fires of human passion, strife and persecution. Every one who, with calm and unbiased mind, will trace the history of the Old Testament—as a book—must be satisfied that it is endowed with divine immortality; and when he reads and devoutly considers its sublime and holy teachings and its rich language, his heart will feel a blessed inspiration and in humility and reverence he will say, this is certainly the word of God.

We will not enter upon the extensive field of Biblical criticism and exposition to consider the question as to the extent of the inspiration of the writers of the Old Testament as we have not the qualifications to discuss the subject in the various phases in which it has been presented. We will not attempt to distinguish between those portions which were originated by inspiration and those that were communicated as revelations. We have the highest authority for believing that "All Scripture is given by inspiration of God," and that the authors "spoke as they were moved by the Holy Spirit." The authors themselves often declared that they spoke and wrote under such divine influence. We have no direct information as to the manner in which this divine influence operated generally upon the minds and hearts of the authors. We fully believe that the Old Testament is the word of God and that the truths, thoughts and facts which it contains were divinely inspired, revealed or controlled with absolute certitude, and that the language used in giving them expression was directly communicated, influenced or sanctioned by the Holy Spirit. Inspiration did not deprive the authors of all individual consciousness, or of their peculiar modes of thought and expression, but kept them from all error while speaking and writing under its influence. Inspiration illumined their minds with infallible light and controlled their genius while they drew appropriate and forcible illustrations of divine truths from the events of the past and present, and when they referred to the manners and customs of their times, and to their vivid perceptions of the objects of the natural world. They were inspired and at the same time many of them had genius of the highest order. They were like the planets of the solar system, differing from each other in magnitude and glory, and yet constituting one harmonious system, revolving round and receiving light from the same great central orb.

The books of the Old Testament, in their diversity of language and imagery, yet oneness of purpose, may well be compared to the rainbow. This beautiful object in nature is "A bow or arch of a circle consisting of all the colors formed by the refraction and reflection of rays of light from drops of rain or vapor appearing in the part of the hemisphere opposite to the sun." The brilliant sunbeams flash in golden beauty from the same source of light, and on the curtain of the storm-cloud paint in various, distinct and nicely blending colors, the bow of God—the sign of His ever-enduring covenant of mercy to man. Thus the light of inspiration, which shone upon the minds and hearts of the Hebrew bards, proceeded from the same source, and was refracted, reflected and separated into different styles of composition by the media through which it passed, and was blended into a harmonious unity glowing with the rich and precious truths and promises of God.

The profound and elevated teachings of the Old Testament were primarily intended for the instruction and guidance of the Hebrews, and within themselves furnish strong evidence that the Hebrews were an intellectual and highly imaginative people. For we must suppose that the knowledge, thought and language used were best suited for the purposes to be accomplished, and were in accordance with the æsthetic tastes and the mental and moral capacities and susceptibilities of the people. God has done nothing imperfectly, and in the wide realms of nature all created things, from the smallest to the greatest, are remarkably adapted to the purposes of their creation, and can we reasonably suppose that this arrangement of order, harmony, beauty and perfection was departed from in His revealed word, intended for the advancement of the high mental and moral nature of man, in which he is most like God.

Our purpose in these lectures is to speak principally of the Old Testament as the repository of the poetry and literature of the ancient Hebrews. Of course we cannot consider it entirely apart from its divine inspiration. We might as well speak of the beauties of the human face without alluding to the soul-light that beams from the eye in eloquent radiance.

We propose to examine this remarkable book by a human standard of excellence, just as a poet and astronomer often regard the brilliant, life-giving warmth and manifold influences of the sun in the wide realms of nature, without specially referring to the omnipotence and goodness of Him who placed it in the heavens and invested it with beneficent influences and controlling power.

The Old Testament, viewed as a human composition, possesses more profound wisdom for the guidance of human action, more instructive and interesting history, and more beautiful and sublime poetry, than all the books of ancient or modern times. We will not enter into the wide fields which it presents for human thought and investigation, but we will confine our attention to those portions which especially contain poetic thought and imagery. And first comes the Pentateuch, venerable for antiquity, profound in wisdom and brilliant with the gems of genius. It was written by a wonderful man. By nature he was endowed with lofty heroism, exalted intellect and genius, and with all those elevated and noble virtues which make men truly great. Forty years of his life were spent at the court of the most highly civilized people of that age, and he was instructed in all their learning and wisdom. Forty years he spent in pastoral occupations amidst the sublime scenery of a mountain wilderness, often holding spiritual communion with Jehovah, and devoutly contemplating the wild grandeur of nature. He also had frequent association with the old Arabian Emirs, who breathed the spirit of liberty, and were instructed by the experiences and long accumulated wisdom of their patriarchal ancestors, and were familiar with the poetic legends and traditions of prehistoric ages.

Most of the language of the Pentateuch is prosaic in form, but still it presents events and scenes which arouse the highest poetic emotions. It is a noble prose epic. How grandly it looms up amidst the shadows of distant centuries, revealing the earliest history and institutions of mankind, and gleaming, as did Sinai of old, with the glory of God. If the Pentateuch and its manifold influences had never existed how different would be the condition of Christendom in its knowledge in history, its culture in literature, its wisdom in civil government and its social and individual enlightenment, prosperity and happiness. It is the deep-laid foundation of that structure of which Christ is the chief corner stone, and which, in the course of centuries, has been reared into the grand temple of Christian civilization. It has not only controlled many of the leading events of history and the civil and religious institutions of mankind, but its thoughts, language and imagery have been inwrought like golden threads in the warp and woof of society, and it furnishes many of the cherished and familiar household words of all classes of men in Christian communities. The old and the young, the rich and the poor, priest and layman, peasant and king, orators, poets, historians, jurists, statesmen and philosophers all obtain treasures of thought and language from this inexhaustible repository of human and divine wisdom. Its poetic elements are interspersed through all of its books, and its melodies are rich and varied like those of the grand orchestra of nature that ranges over every musical note, from the deep-toned bass of the ocean and the thunder to the soft, sweet treble strains of the singing birds.

I feel that my reference to the poetry of the Pentateuch would be very incomplete without calling your special attention to the closing chapters of Deuteronomy, the last utterance of the peculiarly favored friend of God, and the grandest poet and statesman of Israel. They are considered by most Biblical scholars as the finest specimens of Hebrew poetry. The circumstances under which they were written and delivered were grandly sublime and imposing. Moses had been divinely informed that, on account of his sinful conduct and inconsiderate words at Meribah, he would not be allowed to enter the Promised Land. He knew that his end was near, and, with all the tender fondness of a loving father, he was anxious to secure the future welfare of his erring people. By divine direction he had chosen Joshua as his successor, and he was about to deliver his parting blessings and his earnest and eloquent warnings and entreaties to the nation which he had organized and long watched with jealous care. "His eye was not dim nor his natural force abated;" and his wisdom and genius were enlarged and elevated by the experiences of more than a century of years, and illumined by vivid prophetic visions of coming glories. As the servant of Jehovah he had delivered His people from the house of bondage; he had passed with them through the deep caverns of the obedient sea; he had stood alone in the inner audience chamber of awful Sinai and talked "face to face" with his Sovereign Lord; he had conducted His people through the various scenes, dangers and difficulties of their long desert pilgrimage, and had given them beneficent laws, a magnificent religious ritual and free institutions. Nearly all the associates of his earlier years had died in the eventful journey. The voices of the wise elders and counselors whom he had first chosen were silent; Miriam, his much loved and gifted sister, had been buried at Kadesh; and Aaron, who had been his eloquent spokesman, slept in a lonely grave amidst the solitudes of Mt. Hor. Young and vigorous Israel were about to pass over Jordan and possess the "goodly land" which he would never enter, but which he would soon see in his last earthly beatific vision, and then God and the angels would place him in that mountain sepulchre which was forever to remain unknown. There his body sleeps, and the winds and storms of the ages have ever sang his requiem, and the sentinel sun and stars, in ceaseless march, have watched and guarded the ashes of the mighty dead.

As Moses thus stood in holy contemplation before the veil of the tabernacle, and surveyed the white tents of his beloved Israel, extending far over the plains of Moab, "as gardens by the river's side," and while his memory was glowing with the vivid recollections of the eventful past, and while his clear eye of prophecy was resting on visions of mingled gloom and glory in the future, is it to be wondered that his elevated and inspired genius and noble heart should have conceived grand and glorious poetic thoughts which he uttered in language of tearful pathos, rhythmic beauty and lofty sublimity.

For four hundred and fifty years—with the exception of the book of Job—the Pentateuch constituted the only literature of the Hebrews of which we have any definite knowledge. In every period of their history it was regarded with the highest veneration. It was the book of the sacred covenant—the law and constitution of their nation. Its teachings directed their public worship and private devotion, it regulated all civil affairs and social and domestic relations, and was the subject of constant study and devout meditation. We may well conceive that a people so thoroughly imbued with the elevated sentiments and language of their great law-giver, historian and poet must have been animated in a high degree with his lofty spirit and sublime genius.

To show the inuflence of the genius and writings of Moses in transforming the character of his people, we will briefly refer to their early history. A few families of shepherds and husbandmen—all the descendants of Jacob—went down to the land of Goshen. The enervating climate and the corrupt civilization of Egypt, and hard bondage, made the descendants of the free and noble old patriarchs a degenerate and servile people. They had lost their nomadic liberty, and were not yet animated with the higher spirit of freedom, inspired by national unity and independence. The eloquence of Aaron, the poetic earnestness of Miriam, and the God-like wisdom and power of Moses, manifested by wondrous miracles, were all required to make them fly even from the house of cruel bondage. Like a timid herd of slaves, they stood trembling with fear on the shore of the sea, when they heard the noise of the chariot wheels and the advancing march of Pharaoh's hosts. When, by a wonderful deliverance, they reached in safety the other shore they sang the pean of a victory which their courage had not won. When they had encountered the wild sons of Amalek the valor and example of Joshua was not sufficient to urge them on to battle for self preservation until the uplifted hands of Moses, as he invoked divine aid, nerved their hearts, which had quailed under a slight disaster. When the bondage of Egypt and the hardships and privations of the wilderness were behind them, and before them was the Promised Land, consecrated by the graves and memories of their forefathers, flowing with milk and honey, rich in pastures and olive groves, and abounding with perennial streams and the purple clusters of the vines of Eshcol, they listened to the timid spies and shrank from a conflict with the giant sons of Anak, although Jehovah had led them so far through every danger and difficulty, and had so frequently manifested His beneficence and wondrous power. All of the servile and degenerate Hebrews perished in the wilderness, but the teachings of Moses and the stern discipline of a long desert pilgrimage infused into their descendants the spirit of freedom and the vigor of a new national life, and made a nation of conquering heroes. They crossed the Jordan and for seven years were victorious, and with strong hand recovered the land of their ancestors. Then, under the influence of their civil and religious institutions, they became an agricultural and pastoral people, unaggressive and pacific, but strong in defensive valor. They developed the force and beauty of the domestic and social virtues and the principles of individual and national freedom, and surrounded and commingled everything with their elevated religious faith.

The other historical books of the Old Testament furnish a brief and meagre outline of the history of the Hebrews during the time of the commonwealth, the kings, the captivity and the restoration. They are written principally in simple prose, but as they furnish a narrative of great and interesting events they often glow with fervid eloquence, and sometimes swell into the highest strains of poetry; and then, in simple and tender pathos, they picture scenes of pastoral and domestic contentment and repose that gleam like sunshine amidst the shadows of a rich and varied landscape.

The Hebrews, during the commonwealth, were sometimes conquered, and their spirit of freedom temporarily subdued, but during that period they enjoyed long intervals of peace, prosperity and happiness and they were a brave and imperial race, and in moral and intellectual culture and social advancement were far ahead of other contemporary nations. Their subjugation was always a judgment of Jehovah for their sins and rebellion against the government which He had formed. When they returned to their sacred allegiance their spirit of freedom was revived and they were invested with irresistible strength and indomitable courage.

We will refer to one incident in the history of the commonwealth which shows the poetical susceptibility of the Hebrews.

They were subjugated by Jahin, king of Canaan, and his tyranny and power for a time subdued their spirit and they manifested but little disposition to

> "Strike for their altars and their fires,
> For God and their native land."

But the poetic voice of Deborah, from beneath her palm tree dwelling, sounded like a slogan to the listless tribes and rallied them into an army of brave and stalwart warriors, who rested not until they had won victory and freedom. The triumphal ode of Deborah is one of the grandest peans that ever rang in the ears of conquerors. She was well named "A Mother in Israel," as she knew how to rouse and nerve the hearts of her people to accomplish great and glorious deeds.

We will not speak of the achievements of Gideon, Jephthah and Manoah's wondrous son, or refer specially to the military exploits of that heroic age, briefly but graphically described in the Old Testament. We love not the poetry of battle and carnage, as it tells of human passions and strifes, of sufferings and sorrows. To us the martial notes of the trumpet and drum have no pleasing music, while we rejoice in the melody of "flutes and soft recorders" that breathe with the harmonies of pastoral and domestic joys, and our spirit is calmed into reverence and rapt devotion by the sweet, soft voice of sacred song.

It is pleasant to leave the poetry of the battle field and contemplate a book that is full of the gentle and tender pathos of human life and pure affection.

The book of Ruth is called, even by the mocking and scoffing Voltaire, "a gem of oriental history." It was the production of Samuel, the last of the Judges of Israel, and one of the purest, wisest and best men who adorn the records of the chosen people. His infant heart and mind were inspired by the pious teachings of the poetic and saintly Hannah. As a child prophet he talked with Jehovah, and his youthful imagination was illumined and beautified by the splendid ceremonial services of the tabernacle at Shiloh.

The book of Ruth is one of the sweetest poems that ever was written. In the sacred canon it is placed between the narratives of the wars of the Judges and of the bloody and wicked period of the Kings. It is like a little star gleaming in quiet and silvery beauty between two storm clouds fierce with the thunder and gleaming with the lightning, or it may be compared to a soldier's song of home, heard by the bivouac fire in the solemn night, while he rests from a day of carnage, and dreams not of a yet more dreadful morrow. The incidents in this book occurred long before they were recorded, and existed as a legend in the homes of Palestine, and must have cheered and delighted the women of Israel when recited in social and domestic intercourse or on occasions of festivity and joy. The story is a pleasing and pathetic idyl, and presents many lovely scenes of oriental primitive life. In it three charming characters are exquisitely delineated. We see Naomi driven by famine into the idolatrous country of Moab where she lost her husband, fortune and children. Her dark misfortunes of poverty and bereavement were lightened and brightened by calm resignation, and she poured all the wealth of her affections upon her gentle and devoted daughter-in-law. In Boaz we see a noble type of warm-hearted and generous manhood, ever ready to succor the weak, poor and sorrowing with the kindest courtesies and open-handed charity. With what tender sympathy and admiration do we contemplate the young, modest, trustful and beautiful Ruth leaving her kindred and country from a strong sense of filial duty, and that she might dwell beneath the sheltering wings of the Lord God of Israel. The scene between Naomi and her two daughters-in-law—as old, poor and bereaved, she was on her way to return to the land of Judah, friendless and alone—is full of simple and exquisite beauty, and excels in pathetic tenderness and loving devotion the immortal scene of the parting of Hector and Andromache at the Scæan gate when the peerless Trojan hero went forth to battle for the freedom and safety of his kindred and country.

How instructing and encouraging are the simple recitals of Ruth's trials and "rich recompense of reward." The whole book is full and overflowing with poetry, and wakes the sweetest emotions in every heart that loves the gentle, tender and beautiful, and appreciates the joy and bliss of home. It may well be compared to a little fountain in a sequestered dell, surrounded with verdure and overhung with festooned leaves and flowers, and with gentle music ever pouring forth its pure, sweet and refreshing waters. The life history of every pure and holy woman is a beautiful poem. It may never be written on earth, but its sweetness will linger long in many loving hearts, and it will surely find its way to heaven and be recorded in the "Book of Life."

The Book of Esther is usually associated in the mind of Bible readers with the Book of Ruth, as both contain histories of women whose names have given titles to books in the sacred canon. The book has always been highly esteemed by the Jews; and although it does not contain the name of God, they included it in the sacred canon as an important part of their history, in showing the providential dealings of God with their nation. I shall not refer to the various opinions which have been entertained by Biblical critics and expositors as to the claims of canonicity the author and the age when this book was written, as such questions are foreign to the purposes of my lectures. I only refer to it as evidence of a fact which I will hereafter more fully consider—that the spirit of Hebrew poetry became extinct soon after the Captivity. This book does not contain a single rhythmic line or poetic sentiment. It was evidently written by a Jew of post-exilian times, who had none of the poetic spirit of his ancestors. If the old poetic spirit had existed among the people the incidents recorded were well calculated to call forth the finest poetic sentiment and language. Esther was a remarkably beautiful and accomplished woman. She was elevated from a subject race to the throne of an empire which extended from the Indus to Ethiopia and contained one hundred and twenty-seven provinces; and her court blazed with all the splendors of oriental wealth and magnificence; and more than all, her exalted heroism and patriotism must have filled the hearts of her rescued people with devoted love, high admiration and the intense feelings of national pride, thankfulness and joy. These feelings must have existed, but the people had lost the spirit which glowed in the heart of Moses, sounded from the timbrels of Miriam, and thrilled with melody David's harp and Isaiah's lyre. The subsequent history of Esther is unknown. She has a place in the Bible, but her name is not interwoven in the garlands of immortal song. What a striking contrast is presented in the history of Ruth, who lived in the pastoral and poetic age. She, too, was beautiful, but her beauty was of that simple and spiritual type that nestles with love in the inmost heart and breathes celestial harmonies. She was poor and an alien among an exclusive and clannish people, intensely proud of their lineage. And yet her life-history is the sweetest and tenderest idyl in the world's literature—from her sprang the royal and sacred line of David, and her name is enrolled in the immortal lineage of the Prince of Peace.

The Book of Job is the most wonderful production in literature. Written in the wilderness, far back in the deep solitudes of time, it still remains unique and solitary in the world of letters. For more than thirty-five centuries it has stood in archaic majesty, like the pyramids in the silence and solitude of the desert, but ever gleaming with sunlight or with the splendors of unclouded night. This book is without a parallel in human literature, it is unimitated and inimitable. It is more than a parable or an allegory. It is a glowing history, a grand, inspired epic, intended to "vindicate the ways of God to man." The genius of the writer was not trammeled by ritualistic institutions, or artificial rules of composition, or by the manners and customs and prejudices of any particular form of national life. He was as free in thought as the air of his wild mountain home, and he breathed the simple and yet majestic spirit of a remote patriarchal age, and often rose to the highest strains of impassioned eloquence and poetry. The answer of the Lord to Job out of the whirlwind is the sublimest poem ever read by man. The grandest notes of the Cecilian organ would be but a poor accompaniment to that sublime anthem that once swelled out from the glittering bosom of the storm-cloud and mingled with the deep reverberating peals of the thunder. The poetic treasures of this book have been very elaborately considered by most writers upon Hebrew poetry. It contains sublime pictorial scenes and is full of the fire and magnificence of poetic thoughts that throb with energetic life and flow in rich cadences along the rhythmic lines. The inspired genius of the writer sweeps through eternity, its range is as wide as the universe and seems to penetrate celestial infinitude and catch the music of the stars as in rejoicing march they move along their serene pathways in everlasting splendors.

The limits of this lecture will not allow me to linger amidst the gorgeous imagery and oriental splendors of this book. The author is unknown. The age in which he lived and the grave where he was buried cannot be marked out, but his production is an enduring monument of his genius and wisdom; and the consolations and joys which he has given to sorrowing and suffering humanity will hallow his name in eternal remembrance. His genius will ever be held in admiration by men of cultivated tastes for its suggestiveness and richness. It is higher and bolder than any other human effort. Its daring flight may be compared to that of the eagle which builds its nest upon the mountain crag, looks with undazzled eye on the brightness of the sun, and in the gladness of freedom and power, mounts above the clouds, and on strong unwearied wings moves in safety upon the storm, or in far, rapid flight sweeps over the deserts and the seas.

LECTURE XII.

THE PSALMS. THE SONG OF SONGS. PROVERBS.

We feel constrained by the fascination of the subject to dwell at some length upon the character and poetry of David. He may well be called the sweetest singer of Israel. His history itself is a wonderful poem, full of striking, varied and brilliant incidents. We see him first as a shepherd boy guarding his father's flock in the quiet valleys of Bethlehem, and then bowing before the venerable prophet and judge to receive on his young brow the consecrated annointing oil of sovereignty; then as a youthful warrior, with stone and sling, winning the deliverance of his people when the bravest in Israel had faltered; then he is the son-in-law and poet-laureate of his king; then a fugitive, wandering in the wilderness of Engedi and hiding in desert caves; then we see him on the throne, surrounded by wise counselors, ruling over the united kingdom, and, under the lion banner of the tribe of Judah, his great captains lead victorious armies into the rock fortresses of Edom, and storm through the breached walls of Rabbath-Ammon; and then, with rent robes, uncovered head and bleeding feet, we see him weeping and flying from his home before his traitorous and ungrateful son.

His domestic life presents as many beautiful scenes and strange contrasts as his public career. He exhibited the highest genius and chivalry, the loftiest patriotism and purest friendship, the noblest emotions and most tender sympathies and affections; and then he was guilty of duplicity, ingratitude and the darkest vices and crimes.

But the defects of his character are like spots upon the sun; and in the splendor of his genius, the elevation of his piety, the nobility of his soul and in the deep sincerity of his penitence, we forget the errors and weaknesses of his humanity and hail him as one of the noblest and grandest of the sons of men, and acknowledge him as worthy of his high renown and the favor of God.

Although in the poems of his life-history there is such a commingling of brightness and shadow the poems of his genius are sacred and immortal. The harp he loved so well and touched so skilfully had a wide compass of tone; sometimes swelling in strains of the highest grandeur, then ringing with exultant and joyous harmonies, and then breathing out the low, sweet, tremulous notes of humility, love and penitence.

We will not attempt anything like a critical analysis of the Psalms, or make selections from their storehouse of poetic beauties and abounding heart-treasures. We will take only a brief synthetic view of their literary excellencies and refer to some of their most obvious and general characteristics.

They were written by various authors during different ages of the Hebrew state, and are a condensed history of the political, social and religious opinions and feelings of that people. As David composed a large number of these national and religious songs, which are so eloquent and spiritual in language and sentiment, and collected others that were in existence during his reign and adapted them to the temple service, the whole collection is often styled the Psalms of David. He was certainly a prince among his lyrical brethren, and these spiritual productions of inspiration and genius could scarcely be honored with a nobler name.

The Book of Psalms in the Hebrew is styled the "Book of Praises," and is justly entitled to that appellation, as it is full of ascriptions of goodness, mercy, power majesty and dominion to Jehovah. It is also full of expression of pathos, social and domestic love, lofty patriotism, sublime thought and glowing sympathy with the scenery and varied voices of nature. We will not compare them with those divine and inimitable messages of Him who spake as never man spake, but with these exceptions, the Psalms are the sweetest, purest and richest offerings of thought, emotion, reverence and adoring love that the human mind and heart have ever brought to Jehovah's footstool.

The Psalms are as comprehensive and varied as the feelings and emotions of human life—they are the very breathings of the soul. In them may be found every species of Hebrew poetry, and they are remarkably rich in beautiful imagery and illustrations taken from nearly every object in nature, and from nearly every condition of life. They may be compared to a harp of numerous strings, differing in tone, and touched with various fingers, and yet no discordant notes mingle with their combined and multitudinous melodies. They are said to contain "the whole music of the human heart swept by the hand of its Maker."

Bishop Horne says, "The Psalms are an epitome of the Bible adapted to the purposes of devotion," and they are full of the prophetic light and glory of the Gospel. The Psalms are the voices of the ancient Church, in which are uttered its gladness and its glory, its penitence and its griefs, its hopes and its praises. They are still the voices of the Church of God. The various denominations of Christendom may differ as to the doctrinal teachings of the Bible, and as to the rites and ceremonies of worship, but all, with harmonious consent, adopt the Psalms as the voices of Christian life. They constitute a bond of Christian union—sacred and immortal—binding the Churches into a grand catholic unity. They also link Christian hearts with the sympathetic chords of memory, with the glorious men of the old dispensation, and thus perpetuate a vital spiritual union between the living and the dead of God's children which will be continued in all succeeding generations, and thus form a connection between the Church Militant and the Church Triumphant.

I cannot refrain from referring to two familiar facts which especially hallowed and glorified the Psalms with celestial radiance and the beauty of holiness. They are full of prophecies of our Saviour and foreshadowed his Gospel, but those are not their highest glory. He sang one with his disciples at the sad and loving communion of the first Lord's Supper, and with his dying breath, and in the hour of his deepest humiliation and agony, he uttered a sentence of the Psalms from the cross. These were their crowning glories. Need I say more of their spiritual beauties? I will make a general summary. They were inspired by the Holy Spirit, breathed through the lips of holy men—thus mingling divinity with humanity; they were illumined with the light of evangelical prophecy and sanctified with exceeding glory by the approval of our Saviour. Thus they were consecrated and fitted to prepare Christian hearts for the trials, sorrows and joys of earthly life, and then to join in the heavenly songs and hallelujah's of the angels and seraphim as they touch their golden harps in the eternal realms of glory.

As literary productions, judged by the standards of human excellence, we think that we can truthfully say that the Psalms, taken all in all, are the sweetest, the tenderest and most sublime lyrics to be found in literature; and they have exerted the highest and holiest influences upon the happiness, culture and progress of mankind. There is no poetry like the Psalms. They have a living beauty and depth of pathos which can never be excelled and will always wake the highest and holiest harmonies of the human heart. They indeed are immortal. The

Iliad, the Æneid, the Divina Commedia and the Paradise Lost are as immortal as human language, but when they perish the Psalms will be sung by the angels and redeemed ones in Paradise, for they are the songs of God. For more than a thousand years they were the glory of Zion and made glad the City of the Great King. In the magnificent temple service how grandly did they swell in choral joy as they mingled with the music of psaltery and harp swept by the hands of Korah's tuneful sons. They fired the genius of the ancient prophets as they poured forth their sublime rhapsodies to rebellious Israel and disobedient Judah. They gladdened the solitude of the simple Hebrew shepherd as he led his flock through the green pastures and beside the still waters of his heaven-blest land, and the dark-eyed daughters of Zion knew no sweeter minstrelsy than that which the royal minstrel sang. They called up sweet memories and bright hopes in the sad hearts of the captive Israelites, as weeping they sat by the dark waters of Babel, and in secret tuned their plaintive harps to sing one of the loved songs of their fatherland. When the great Macedonian conqueror came sweeping like a besom of distruction over the decaying empires of the East, these sacred songs were soon translated into the beautifully poetic language of Greece, and were scattered like precious gems over all the nations of the Orient. They were the admiration of the disbelieving Gentile, and roused the patriotic pride and religious zeal of the self-exiled Jew in the land of the Ptolemies, among the classic groves of Greece and amid the proud palaces and temples of the seven-hilled city of the Tiber.

The Psalms often engaged the attention of Christ and his disciples as they held holy converse in the wilderness and on the mountains of Judea, and while wandering among the fruitful valleys of Samaria and the Jordan, while preaching and working miracles in the towns and cities of Galilee, and resting on the bosom of Genesareth as she slept in beauty beneath her sunbright or starry skies, or while their little vessel was tossed in fury by the angry and crested waves. They were the cradle songs that cheered the infant Church—they were the martyr's chant in the bloody amphitheatre and rose to heaven amidst the wild and cruel shouts of heathen persecutors. They sounded like blest spirit voices through Mediæval darkness and they were the vesper and matin hymns of the pious Waldenses in their mountain temples. They kindled the enthusiasm of the chivalric crusader as he pressed through the arrows of the pestilence and the storm of battle to the rescue of the Holy Sepulchre. They were the defiant notes of the bold Reformers while they roused Europe from spiritual lethargy and disregarded the pealing thunders of the Vatican. In wild and thrilling cadences they echoed from the glens and caverns of Scotland, where the stern Covenanters, fearing naught but God, were preparing to die for the purity and sanctity of their faith; and they were the pæans of the iron veterans of Cromwell, as in victory they trod the battle-fields of freedom. They were the farewell strains of the Pilgrim Fathers as they left their kindred and country, and in holy raptures they rose from the deck of the Mayflower as she breasted the wintry billows of the stormy Atlantic, and they broke the stillness of the American wilderness and hallowed the land of our fathers.

The Psalms have been heard amidst the icy palaces of the frozen North where the Aurora-Borealis continually is glowing; in the distant isles of the tropic seas where evergreen woodlands bud and blossom beneath the pathway of the sun; and they have often cheered and strengthened the weary pilgrim amidst the silence and solitude of the desert. Like angel visitants, with glad music on their wings, they have entered the stately homes of the great and the humble cottages of the poor, and illumined with heavenly radiance the fading eyes of dying saints. They have nerved the heart of the suffering Christian hero in his lonely dungeon and sustained fainting martyrs at the fiery stake.

They have expressed the deepest emotions of worshipers in the mosques of Islam, the Churches of Christendom and the secret chambers of penitence and prayer. They have been attuned to the noblest melodies of earth; have been associated with the purest affections and dearest memories of home, and everywhere have been the language of the human heart as it poured forth its earnest longings and brightest hopes of heaven.

The Psalms have been translated into more than two hundred different languages; have added beauty and vitality to all Christian literature, and they are the sacred fountains from which great bards have drank the inspiring waters which made them immortal and gave to their genius the magic power that thrilled the mystic strings of the human heart.

Wherever the foot of civilized man has trod the pathways either of ambition or commerce these olden songs have gone with their consolations and joys and conferred more precious treasures than wealth or fame. They have gone even further than man's greed for power and gain, they have been borne by Christian missionaries and exerted their divine influences in pestilential climes and savage wilds where the light of civilization has scarcely shone. Like the sunshine and dews of heaven they seem to have fallen on nearly every land of the earth.

Although the Psalms have passed through the revolutions and changes of three thousand years, which have wrecked nearly all the productions and memorials of man's pride, intellect and ambition, they have in spirit much of the vitality and freshness which they had when they first gushed from the hearts and minds of the old Hebrew bards among the beautiful hills and valleys of the Promised Land. We fully believe that the time will come at no distant day when these songs of Zion will be heard in every home and every tongue will sing their praises unto Israel's God.

How profusely has the prolific and inspired genius of Solomon scattered the treasures of wisdom and the gems of poesy over the sacred page. The "Song of Songs" was evidently written in youth, when the heart of the poet was full of the exhuberant love and joyousness of innocent life. It is a paradisaical idyl breathing the loves of the pure in heart. Among the Jews and in the Christian Church it has been regarded as an allegorical representation of the mystic union and tenderness existing between Jehovah and Israel—Christ and his Church. It is also supposed to be an image of Eden before sin had entered its hallowed precincts and marred its heavenly beauty. Where the first human pair dwelt in hymeneal bliss; where the soft and gentle North wind and South wind caused the odors of spices to flow out; where the gladsome fountains and murmuring groves joined in ceaseless and harmonious concert, and the little throats of the singing birds were almost bursting with melody, and the sunlight was sporting with joy over green lawns, luscious fruits, blooming flowers and sparkling musical waters, while the voice of God uttered continual benedictions.

This book is the most complete and artistic poem in the Bible and it is by far the most mystical. It differs somewhat in thought and style from all the other books of the sacred canon. We will not attempt to expound its spiritual meaning and purposes. Upon these questions we accept the general opinion of the Church without objection. As a literary production this book is full of rhythm and the choicest poetic imagery. Nature is presented in the richest and loveliest garbe of spring, and abounding in everything calculated to contribute to the exquisite enjoyments of refined and elegant tastes, and the persons represented are high ideals of gracefulness, symmetry and beauty animated in their endearments and caresses by a tender, pure and delicate love. It well deserves the title given it in the Hebrew language, which signifies "The most beautiful song."

The Book of Proverbs contains some of the precious thoughts and experiences of the Hebrew people, collected and arranged into beautiful literary mosaics by the inspired genius of Solomon. The Hebrews were "a kingdom of priests and a holy nation" unto the Lord, and His spirit dwelt among them and sanctified their hearts and enlightened their minds with divine thoughts and holy emotions, that were expressed in social and religious intercourse in beautiful and appropriate language. We fully believe that God inspired the writers of the Bible as special messengers for communicating His revealed word to mankind, but we also believe that His Holy Spirit has, in every age, dwelt among His believing people, illumining their minds and hearts with holy thoughts and emotions, which have been expressed in language approved by Him. As God, in providence is ever sowing the germs of trees, flowers and verdure in the natural world, which His messengers and agents—the light, rain, dews and other forces—are continually rearing into fruitfulness, bloom and fragrance for the delight and enjoyment of mankind; we may well believe that His Holy Spirit has in every age illumined the minds and hearts of His people with thoughts and expressions of beauty and holiness that come from the heavenly home to cheer and to bless. We are taught to pray for the wisdom and guidance of the Holy Spirit in our thoughts, words and actions.

There are many productions in Christian literature, and many songs used in the church service which elevate and brighten our faith and devotion and fill our hearts with holy raptures, and why may we not believe that these productions of saintly men sprang from divine illumination and were not the mere creations of human genius? We believe that the Book of Proverbs was written and arranged under the guidance of divine inspiration and contains many of the maxims of Hebrew wisdom and experience, the products of the popular mind influenced by the Holy Spirit.

The proverbial style was very common among the Hebrews, and is an evidence of their quick mental and moral perceptions and energy of thought. We find this style of composition in the Apocryphal Books the Talmud and other Rabbinical writings of a subsequent age.

The Book of Proverbs is one of the most instructive and polished books in the Old Testament. Its language is terse and elegant and full of the beauties of poetry. Its teachings have been apt and forcible in every age and in every language, as they are full of truth and well adapted to the various conditions of human life, and have conferred inestimable blessings upon mankind.

All nations have their proverbs, expressing with beauty and force, social, political and moral truths applicable to the intercourse of men in the various walks of life and their wisdom is sanctioned by human experience. Many of them are the productions of men of genius and sages, while others float like waifs on the currents of popular feeling and intelligence, and cannot be traced to the individual minds and circumstances from which they sprang.

Most of the precious metals used by mankind were extracted from rude and shapeless ores taken with great labor and skill from quartz, slate and granite veins in deep mines, but many precious gems and grains and nuggets of gold have been accidentally found by the wayside, in sequestered valleys and in rivulets and streams. The great mass of human knowledge and wisdom has been accumulated by the patient and laborious study and investigations of sages and philosophers, but in proverbial and poetic literature we often find brilliant intellectual gems and many treasures of knowledge which unknown sons of genius placed in the wide fields of human thought. Some of the finest thoughts and expressions in the literature of every nation are the spontaneous products of the minds and hearts of the people in the ordinary intercourse of social and domestic life. They are the amber, pearls and grains of gold which the strong and restless ocean of popular feeling and sentiment has thrown up from its depths and cast upon the shore, and they were collected by men of taste and genius and skilfully inwrought into the rich texture of literature. Upon careful examination it will be found that many national proverbs which teach moral, social and political truths derived much of their wisdom, vitality, epigrammatic force and beauty from the influence of the old Hebrew mind.

From this brief and imperfect consideration of some of the books of the Old Testament may we not well conclude that they are worthy of our constant and careful study, even as literary productions, as they contain so much bright, pure, sublime and beautiful language, imagery and thought.

LECTURE XIII.

The Prophecies.

In the course of our investigations in Hebrew poetry we have reached the books of the Prophets, and a very cursory examination will show that they are highly poetical and full of impassioned eloquence and grandeur of imagery. Before separately considering these books we will briefly refer to the characters of the Prop het bards and the circumstances by which they were surrounded and influenced, for the purpose of showing that there existed many natural causes well calculated to elevate and intensify their genius.

In the sacred history of Israel we find many persons who had the gift of prophecy and gave utterance to sublime thoughts in language highly poetical. We find a striking instance in Baalam, the son of Beor. He seems to have had some knowledge of the true God, derived from the old patriarchal dispensation, but he had mingled with this religious belief the superstitions of pagan idolatry. His prophecy is one of the most elegant and beautiful pieces of poetic composition to be found in any literature. It flowed from his unwilling lips under the influence of divine inspiration and was recorded by Moses, and the style may have received some of its glow and brilliancy from the inspired genius of the great poet and lawgiver. We forbear to make reference to the utterances of some other prophets mentioned in the Old Testament, as we desire to confine our attention to the productions of those writers who strictly belong to the " goodly fellowship of the Prophets." They were chosen by God as instruments to explain some of his dealings in the past and reveal, to some extent, His will, His plans and purposes in the future government and salvation of His spiritual Isreal.

The roll of the prophet writers was opened about the reign of Uzziah, and at that time the condition of the tribes of Israel was well calculated to excite in the mind of a patriotic Hebrew painful solicitude and apprehension for the future welfare of his nation. The tribes had long been divided into the kingdoms of Israel and Judah, and were discordant and beligerent; and being thus weakened by internal disorders and dissensions the country was often wasted by civil wars and the invasions of neighboring nations. The people had also greatly degenerated in moral and religious character, and were yielding to the corrupting influences of paganism.

The Prophets were pure and high-toned patriots and all the energies and faculties of their minds and hearts were aroused in the effort to save their beloved country from impending ruin. Thus their genius and affections were kindled to the brightest glow as they pleaded with their erring and wayward countrymen and denounced their cruel enemies.

There are two words in the Hebrew language of nearly synonymous import which are often used to designate the prophet, and in our language signifies " One who sees." The Prophets might well be called *seers* for magnificent visions of the past, the present and the future were by the inspiration of God presented to their spiritual intuition. They may not have understood the full import of the divine communications and the scope of the visions they witnessed, but under the guidance of the Holy Spirit they described the scenes with the highest poetic vividness. The contemplation of such scenes must have had great influence in enlarging their minds as they ranged through an extensive field of vision. They saw the connection and continuity of time—the past, the present and the future. They beheld God in histroy and prophecy working out wondrous plans, all connected and controlled by a general purpose. We can look back and see what has been accomplished. We know that the waves which the ancient nations started on the great ocean of human existence have continued to roll ever onward, and we can well believe that they will never cease until they break on the shores of eternity when time shall be no more. But the Prophets saw many of these events in the womb of the future. In the light of history we will refer to some of the scenes and events with which the Prophets were familiar or saw in the vivid visions of prophecy.

During the period of Hebrew national life the great oriental monarchies performed their part in the wondrous drama of universal history. There was Egypt in the pride of her power—even then hoary with age, without its decrepitude and decay, rich in the annals and accumulations of centuries, the cradle of human civilization—the fountain of philosophy, science and art; covered with splendid cities and those stupendous monuments of human enterprise, energy and skill, which even in ruins, have astounded with their magnitude and magnificence the most enlightened nations of the modern world.

In the East were Nineveh and Babylon, the magnificent emporiums of the Mesopotamian valley, with hundreds of palaces and temples "shining in silver and gold, as splendid as the sun"; surrounded with well-watered orchards, vineyards, gardens and meadows sparkling in beauty and fertile in abundance. In territorial extent these cities were almost kingdoms, and were enclosed with extensive, massive and lofty walls surmounted with more than a thousand strong towers. They were filled with an intelligent and busy population: they received tribute from the submissive nations of a continent; their armies were almost countless and were strengthened by discipline and repeated conquests; statements of their wealth and magnificence seem fabulous, and many of the structures which they reared were regarded as among the wonders of the world. They had histories venerable for antiquity and rich in intellectual achievements and martial renown, and they could trace their line of kings almost to the Deluge. The stories of these two empire cities read like the extravagant fictions of an oriental dream. There the descendants of Shem, Ham and Japheth separated to re-people the flood-swept world, and there the Chaldean magi first with intelligent eyes mapped out the constellations, tracked the planets in their courses, pointed out the beauties of the earth's zodiacal girdle, and read some of the mysteries and eloquence of the radiant stars. They are to us the lands of ruins, mystery, poetry and old romance, and they must in their power and glory have been wondrous to the shepherds of Palestine.

On the Southern border of the Holy Land the wild sons of Ishmael were fulfilling their prophetic destiny, and were roaming over the deserts in that unrestrained freedom that was ever to remain unconquerable by man or time. There too the stern children of Edom carved their fortresses and temples in the bosom of the mountains and built their dwellings among the cliffs of the rocks, on the eyries of the eagles.

To the North beneath the shadows of Lebanon the queenly cities of Tyre and Sidon sat in sumptuous magnificence by the sea. They had planted industrious and prosperous colonies on every shore of the Mediterranean, and their stately triremes had gathered wealth from the " Isles of the Gentiles," and in adventurous commercial enterprise had sailed beyond the pillared gates of the distant Atlantic. They had sent their cunning craftsmen and skilled artisans to rear the grand structures of religion, pride, wealth and ambition in every land and fill them with the beautiful productions of imitative art; while their merchant princes, robed in purple and fine linen, spent their hours of repose in elegantly adorned palaces and gardens, and lavished treasures in the excesses of voluptuousness.

I will not refer at any length to the giant structures of Bashan, Moab and Ammon, or to the five cities of warlike Philistia—rich from abundant harvests and from their extensive commerce with the "spicy shore of Arabie the blest."

All these nations and peoples were, at times, the enemies and oppressors of Israel, and the Prophets foresaw their coming doom. They saw in visions the fierce legions of the Persians, the Babylonians, the Greeks, the Romans, the Saracens and the Ottomans sweep in desolating course over the fertile valley of the Nile— leaving no vestige of old Egypt's greatness and glory but Titanic ruins and the time-defying pyramids They saw Nineveh, the metropolis of the Orient, encompassed by the relentless Medes; then the gates of the river opened and dissolved her walls; then her proudest palace became a vast funeral pyre that consumed the last of her kings; then her nobles were dwelling in the dust and her people were scattered on the mountains. Then they saw her for centuries lying in desolation and "dry like a wilderness." "Flocks lie down in the midst of her." "Hawks and crows nestle in her ruined battlements." "The cormorant and bittern lodge in her upper lintels and sing in the windows." Then the agencies of nature and time slowly cover her grave of oblivion where she sleeps for twenty-five hundred years, when an Englishman "uncovers her cedar work," excavates her palaces and reveals her sculptured history to an astonished world and confirms the truth of divine prophecy.

With what graphic power and gorgeous imagery do the prophets describe their panoramic visions of the downfall of "The Golden City." "The glory of kingdoms and the beauty of the Chaldee's excellence." When we read Isaiah's description of the approach of Cyrus with his multitudinous army, collected from all nations, we can almost hear the rush of the chariots, the trampling of the horses, and the tread of the legions as they gather to the harvest of death. "The noise of a multitude in the mountains like as a great people, a tumultuous noise of the kingdoms, of nations gathered together, the Lord of hosts mustereth the hosts of battle." Then came the disastrous overthrow. When the brightly lighted festal halls of Babylon were ringing with shouts and songs of sinful revelry, a mysterious hand wrote the sentence of doom on the wall before Belshazzar and his courtiers; then from the bed of the river the furious Persians and Medes pour like waves of fire over her palaces and homes. Her gates of brass are broken in pieces and her iron bars cut asunder, and the hidden treasures of secret places become the spoils of conquest. "A sword is upon the Chaldeans and upon the inhabitants of Babylon and upon her princes and upon her wise men," and they are dismayed and "become as women." For several centuries afterwards Babylon was a beacon-light among the nations, sometimes glowing in brightness, but at last every spark of glory died in ashes and she became a heap of ruins, where not even the wild Arabs pitch their tents or the shepherds fold their flocks.

I will only allude to the prophetic doom of Edom, so long buried in the silence and desolation of her mountain grave. I will not attempt to trace the glory and the gloom mingled in the history of Tyre—the city of ten thousand masts, until she sank beneath the waves upon which her proud navies had ridden in commercial triumph. She became a place where the fishermen dry their nets. "A mournful silence now prevails along the shore which once resounded with the world's debate." Many of the visions of prophecy have become the facts and truths of history.

Need I dwell longer in showing that the Hebrew prophetic bards were surrounded by circumstances and were gifted with visions well calculated to develop the highest poetic enthusiasm? If the story of Troy and the valiant Greeks created the splendid diction and imagery of the Iliad, can we be surprised that the magnificent visions of prophecy should have filled the minds and hearts of the Prophet bards with sublime and glorious thoughts and images which under divine inspiration bursted forth in rapturous song?

While the books of the Prophets were so full of rich language, sublime thought and vivid imagery, they were in their teachings to the people the most obscure portions of their literature. This obscurity necessarily resulted from the nature of prophecy. God did not intend to make the future as luminous as the past. He gave only glimpses of His divine purposes that His people might ever be in a condition of earnest expectancy and hope and have their faith in Him brightened and strengthened as He evolved His wondrous plans. The prophecies to the spiritual perceptions of the Hebrew people were like the bright and ever-shining stars in the firmament to their natural vision as they gleamed in surrounding darkness. As to unaccomplished prophecies the Christian world is in the same condition. We cannot understand their meaning until God sees proper to unfold His purposes.

The astronomer with his telescope can range through

the heavens and catch the light of distant planets and stars and discover some of the general laws which regulate their motion, but he can never see their full orbed splendors or attain that infinite knowledge which will enable him to understand fully the celestial mechanism of the universe; to bind the sweet influences of Pleiades, loose the bands of Orion, bring forth Mazzaroth in his season, or guide Arcturus with his sons. We know that the heavenly hosts in their revolving motions are directed by some great central force which God comprehends and controls for His own glory.

Thus, while we read and partially comprehend and appreciate the grand truths and magnificent imagery of the prophecies, we will not attempt to solve the mysteries they present, which have so long bewildered the minds of learned and earnest men. "Canst thou by searching find out God; canst thou find out the Almighty unto perfection." The Prophets were spokesmen for God, and although we cannot fully understand all His utterances, we know that they are true and righteous. Modern science may mislead many earnest investigators after truth, and entangle them in the ingenious cobwebs of its sophestries, but we hope ever to read the Bible with the sincere veneration of a devout worshiper and the simple, undoubting confidence of a child.

We will only glance at the literary excellencies of the prophecies and be content with the spiritual beauties which they display to the eye of an humble faith.

The images of other poets are the tapestries of fancy woven in the aerial loom of genius, while the visions of the Prophet bards were vivid glimpses of grand realities gleaming with the light of inspiration.

A striking characterestic of the Prophet bards is intensity of thought and passionate purpose. The ordinary word for *Prophet* in the Hebrew language signifies "to boil up or gush out like a fountain." The minds and hearts of the Prophets were not trickling, but gushing fountains, from which have flowed streams which have made glad the city of God. We have often thought that there was something grand and imposing in the *personnel* of Elijah and Isaiah which inspired veneration and awe. Their faces must have beamed and their eyes have glowed with celestial light as they uttered their eloquent and impassioned messages to their erring countrymen. They walked so closely with God that they must have caught some of the light of His glory. We know that the face of Moses shone with exceeding brightness when he came down from Mount Sinai with the tables of the law; and we also know that the face of St. Stephen, transfigured by the glorious faith that burned in his soul, "shone like the face of an angel." But upon this subject the word of God is silent, and we have only a few allusions to the personal characters of these wondrous Prophets.

The progress of human destiny has been principally developed by two distinctive classes of men, *great thinkers and great actors*. We might select from the annals of man many examples of each class, but in doing so we would only present lists of immortal names with which you are familiar. The great actors occupy the most prominent place in written history, as the results which they accomplished were more immediate, striking and eventful. But the attentive student of history will not fail to observe that the great thinkers originated, discovered or combined those important political, intellectual, moral, social and physical truths and principles which produced revolutions in States, advancement in science and glory in art, and gave force, energy and power to great actors. Electricity silently and imperceptibly gathers in the clouds and sends forth the thunder-bolts. The Cyclopean forces in nature that work in the deep cavern laboratories of the earth create the earthquake and pour out the fiery streams of the volcano. They have changed the boundaries of continents, furrowed the earth with deep valleys and upheaved the everlasting hills. We often find great actors possessing great intellect, but their thoughts were suggested by sudden emergencies and were required for immediate operations. But abstract thinkers in solitude work out and bring to light in proper connection and continuity the fundamental truths and principles that permanently affect human action and guide and control the various elements of civilization.

Cromwell was a great actor and practical thinker, and elevated England to the front rank among nations, but the truths and principles that enlightened his mind, nerved his heart and strengthened his arm, sprang from the brains and hearts of Luther, Calvin, Knox and Milton, and were by them derived from the Bible. Cromwell died and his dynasty passed away, but the truths and principles promulgated by the great thinkers of Protestantism lie at the foundation of civil and religious freedom and are the intellectual and moral motive powers of advancing civilization.

The French revolution was a grand political and moral volcano, produced by the struggles between antagonistic elements of thought which great thinkers had infused into French society. Napoleon Boneparte was thrown to the surface by the convulsive throes of human passion and strife, and he had the mental power and physical courage to guide for a time the desolating streams of fire and blood that swept over the face of Europe; but he died a captive, far from his native land, in a lonely island, beneath skies that never spread their glorious beauties over France, and the wild winds alone sang his requiem as they swept the harp of the melancholy ocean: but the great truths and principles of civil and intellectual freedom still live and shake the thrones, principalities and powers of Europe. Brave and experienced generals may marshal armies on fields of carnage, and conquer kingdoms which they have deluged with blood and tears, but it is the student, the philosopher, the school master, the minister of God and the enlightened statesman who form aright public opinion and shape the destinies of States, and produce the glorious triumphs and permanent blessings of peace.

In the fields of science and of intellectual culture the great thinkers have no rivals in influence and fame. Bacon, with the safety lamp of experiment, trod with firm and cautious steps through the unexplored labyrinths of science, and taught men how to follow his footsteps. He has well been called the Luther of science, as he led the human mind from the dark and tangled mazes of ancient and scholastic philosophy into the clear light, and pointed out the sure pathway to the shrines of scientific truth.

Copernicus, Galileo and Newton won the trophies of knowledge and their immortal fame in the silent study where on the strong wings of thought their minds soared to the illimitable fields of the celestial world and brought down to earth the knowledge which they had learned amid the golden stars. I might mention Watt, Guttemberg, Faust, Franklin, Fulton, Morse, and hundreds of great thinkers who have conferred inestimable treasures of knowledge upon the world. I will present no further illustrations. The facts are well established that thought is more powerful than force, "the pen is mightier than the sword." The great thinkers of the past are

> "The dead but sceptred sovereigns who still rule
> Our spirits from their urns."

The Hebrew law-givers, prophets and bards were the first great thinkers who started

> "Those thoughts that wander through eternity,"

and produced so many of the invaluable blessings of

Christian civilization, and which now urge mankind onward to a higher, nobler and more spiritual life.

The prophet bards were not only great thinkers, but they were the cheerful and exultant harbingers of the brightest hopes of humanity. In the midst of the moral darkness and misery that overshadowed the world they saw in the distant future the bright day of righteousness for all mankind. The first prophecy was uttered by God in Eden, and foretold a dark and sorrowful life for man, and it also contained the brightest hope of the world, which sheds its light over the succeeding ages.

Through the whole period of Hebrew history this day star of hope cast its reviving and cheering light on the prophecies and seemed to glow with effulgent radiance in the writings of Isaiah. The Prophets were certainly the morning stars of human hope, as they sang together, and their songs were repeated in higher and holier strains in the "gloria in excelsis" of the heavenly hosts over the plains of Bethlehem at the birth of the Prince of Peace.

There is some diversity of opinion as to the manner in which the Prophets received their divine communications and originally delivered them. In the Bible we find instances in which such communications were delivered by an audible voice, and sometimes in visions and in dreams. We are of the opinion that the Prophets had no fixed method of delivery. They spoke when and where God directed. Sometimes their messages were delivered orally and in the very ecstacies of inspiration. Sometimes they were carefully written and then promulgated. They were generally delivered in the courts of the temple, in the palaces of Kings and in the assemblies of the people. The books of the Prophets preserved in the sacred canon were carefully written by their authors under the guidance of the Holy Spirit. These books did not constitute a part of the ritual service of worship until a period long subsequent to the Captivity, but they were read and explained to the people by the priests and Levites and members of the Schools of the Prophets who were the religious instructors before the exile. The familiarity of the people with these sacred books must necessarily have promoted their intellectual and moral culture and operated powerfully upon their imaginations. No nation ever lived in such a condition of expectancy and hope as the Hebrews, and this feeling was increased by the prophet bards. They believed that they would not only receive the highest temporal and spiritual blessings for themselves, but that they were to be the divine agents for bestowing these rich beneficences upon all races and all times.

LECTURE XIV.

The Prophets.

We propose in this lecture briefly to refer to the productions of some of the chief singers in the grand prophetic choir. If we were asked to describe the Alps we would first allude to Mt. Blanc, the monarch of those mountains. Thus we will select Isaiah, the prince among the Prophets. He is properly styled the Evangelical Prophet, as he so harmoniously blends the revelations of the Old and New Dispensations.

Among his brethren he was like Paul among the Apostles. He had a breadth of mental grasp that was superhuman, and his benign catholicity of feeling made him love all the races of men, even to the most distant future. He foresaw more clearly than any other prophet the remote age when there would be a brotherhood of nations,

> " And they shall beat their swords into plough-shares,
> And their spears into pruning hooks,
> Nation shall not lift up sword against nation,
> Neither shall they learn war any more:"

A time when peace, truth, justice, freedom and universal righteousness would exist in the grand community of races; and the will of God be "done on earth, even as it is done in heaven."

Isaiah prophesied for more than sixty years, and yet there seems to have been no abatement in his genius. It shone forth as freshly and brilliantly when he was tremulous with age as it did when he spoke in all the enthusiasm and vehemence of youth. There is an incomparable dignity of sentiment and splendor of diction in his prophecies which have won the admiration even of scoffing infidels. His sublimity of thought and imagery is truly magnificent. He invoked heaven and earth as the hearers of his divine messages, as if they were almost too grand for the contemplation of the human mind. In his inspired raptures he seems to have mounted on a chariot of fire and ascended to those rich fields of poetic thought which mortal foot never again will tread, as he left no mantle behind him to rest upon the shoulders of a successor. From those empyrean heights he surveyed the past and the illimitable future. He pictured not the mere ideal conceptions of genius, but the visions of grand realities as seen with the clear, strong eye of prophecy. Other poets wandered back through the dark vistas of the past to the treasure fields of poetry to gather the rich gems of thought and glowing pictures of the sublime and beautiful; but he stood upon the top of the mountain of the Lord and saw unveiled a grand panorama of coming events. He saw the dark doom of Israel, the Advent of the Messiah, the agonies of Gethsemane and the dread tragedy of Calvary when the Emaculate One was led like a lamb to the slaughter and opened not his mouth. He saw the Church as she stood with lofty heroism amidst the blood and fire of the martyr ages; as she struggled for existence through mediæval ignorance, superstition and bigotry; and then the dawning brightness of future triumphs; and then in glorious perspective down the long vista of the centuries caught glimpses of the splendid meridian day of Christ's millennial reign, and in such rapt moments heard the far off music of the songs which the Seraphim sing. How appropriately may we apply to this prophet one of his own glorious rhapsodies, "How beautiful upon the mountains are the feet of him that bringeth good tidings, that publisheth peace, that publisheth salvation; that saith unto Zion, thy God reigneth."

The most gifted of human painters will never be able

to copy correctly the dawning brightness of the morning, the gorgeous splendors of the evening, or the silvery beauty of the night, all glorious with moon, planets and stars. With his skilful pencil of art he cannot catch all the gleaming light and varying shades of the glowing landscape which God has spread out with infinite variety for the delight and enjoyment of His creatures. He cannot picture the terrific grandeur of the storm embroidered with the glittering arabesques of the lightning, the sublimity of God's mountain temples, or the magnificence of the ocean in the splendors of its vastness and power. The works of God furnish instruction, guidance and models for human genius, and these works may be somewhat imitated but never equalled. Thus it is with the poetry of Isaiah. It is a treasury filled with gems of thought and images of beauty that enrich the productions of genius, but can never be equalled by human effort. His lips were touched by the Seraphim with a live coal from off the altar. In style as well as thought this poetry is sublime and inimitable. It is like the swelling billows of the ocean that roll in liquid and crystal beauty and inspire the mind and heart with feelings of grandeur as they flow on to the distant and unseen shores in united strength, majesty and power.

JEREMIAH.

Nowhere within the range of human literature can be found such touching strains of grief, such pathos of sorrow as those which the mild and patriotic Jeremiah uttered while weeping over the desolation of Zion, and for the slain of the daughters of his people—"for the strong staff broken and the beautiful rod." The life of this Prophet was full of sadness and misfortune. His gentle, tender, sensitive and loving spirit was subjected to the sorest trials. With intense devotion he loved his countrymen, and yet they treated him with the grossest indignities, scorn and cruelty. His country was torn asunder by internal disorders, and he foresaw but could not avert her impending doom. He witnessed the desecration and destruction of the magnificent temple, with its consecrated emblems and shrines and the Holy of Holies. With eyes that were a fountain of tears he beheld the beautiful city of his fathers, which had once been full of people and a princess among the nations as she sat in sackcloth and solitude upon her sacred mountains, mourning for the sorrows and misfortunes of her captive and exiled children. The Lamentations are the weeping melodies of a broken heart whose shattered but still living strings vibrated with wailing agonies. They have well been called the cygnian strains of the old Hebrew muse before she sank into the silence of death amidst the ruins of Israel's freedom and glory.

EZEKIEL.

Ezekiel is usually and properly classed as one of the greater Prophets. He was truly the representative of the spirit of a great people in the hours of their sorest trials and adversities. He was among the first captives who were carried into exile and colonized on the river Chebar. Most of his prophecy was written in the interval between the capture of Jerusalem and the subsequent distruction of the temple of Solomon, which was the final overthrow of the old Hebrew nationality. In natural disposition and spiritual endowments he was a fine type of the Hebrew prophet and he devoted all the vigor and energy of his nature to his great work of instructing, consoling and guiding his fellow-countrymen. The character of his genius and style of composition is finely portrayed by Bishop Lowth:

"Ezekiel is much inferior to Jeremiah in eloquence; in sublimity he is not even excelled by Isaiah; but his sublimity is of a totally different kind. He is deep, vehement, tragical: the only sensation he affects to incite is the terrible; his sentiments are elevated, fervid, full of fire, indignant; his imagery is crowded, magnificent, terrific, sometimes almost to disgust; his language is pompous, solemn, austere, rough and at times unpolished; he employs frequent repetition, not for the sake of grace and elegance, but from the vehemence of passion and indignation."

Bishop Lowth regards Ezekiel as more of an orator than a poet. His writings are certainly deficient in the ease, grace, rythmical elegance and varied and pleasing imagery which distinguished the productions of the older Hebrew bards. His visions are described with a minuteness of detail and sharpness of outline that is not usual in Hebrew poetry or the poetry of any other people. His grand, solemn and magnificent visions could not be depicted without some of the glow of poetry—but it shone like the iridescent spray of the cataract or the phosphorescent gleam of the strong ocean billows. Bishop Lowth remarked that "Isaiah, Jeremiah and Ezekiel, as far as relates to style, may be said to hold the same rank among the Hebrews, as Homer, Simonides and Eschylus among the Greeks."

Ezekiel is the last name on the roll of the great Hebrew bards and his strains peal forth like the notes of a trumpet showing that his free spirit could never be enslaved. With lofty enthusiasm he revealed the dread doom of the enemies of Israel and the grand and glorious destinies of his nation and of future generations. The closing chapters of Ezekiel's prophecy, although, not poetical in structure and language, are highly poetical in imagery. His vision of the sanctuary, and of the mystical river that came from beneath the altar, and continued to widen and deepen as it flowed onward, healing the waters of the sea of death, fertilizing the desert, carrying life wherever it went and fringed with various trees of fadeless verdure and perpetual fruitage, glows with the finest spirit of poetry. The scene in many respects resembles that more gloriously beautiful vision of the celestial city in which the Angel of the Apocalypse showed unto the Beloved Desciple "a pure river of water of life, clear as crystal, proceeding out of the throne of God and of the Lamb." Ezekiel was a noble prophet and patriot and his mind was filled with grand thoughts and sublime visions, but he did not always express them in the rhythmic elegance and beauty of poetry.

The destruction of Solomon's temple with its sacred emblems and splendid and imposing ceremonial services seems to have terminated the golden age of Hebrew poetry. Its transient and flickering glow in after ages was like the gleam of radiance that is often seen on the face of the dying. The Captives carried the Hebrew lyre into exile, but no hand save Ezekiel's ever touched its loftiest chords in the land of bondage. It hung in silence upon the willows, and sometimes in secret its plaintive melodies were awakened when the captives remembered Zion, told the tale of their sorrows and wept. Most of the Captives soon forgot the majestic and musical language which once sounded forth in choral gladness and grandeur the high praises of Jehovah and the beautiful memories and imagery of the Fatherland.

Daniel was a wise and accomplished courtier and statesman, but he was not a poet. To him the future was largely revealed, but he looked upon such visions, not with the vivid enthusiasm of the poet, but with the calm, discriminating and reverential eye of a devout philosopher watching the progressive development of human destiny. When we compare the writings of Daniel and most of the book of Ezekiel with the productions of the older bards and prophets of Israel we are reminded of two of the schools of modern painting. The Flemish artists in their great productions depict natural objects and ideal conceptions with distinct and exact outlines which claim admiration for the skill and precision of art, but they excite none of those thrilling and elevating ecstacies which are felt while gazing at the softly beautiful landscapes of Claude, the graceful elegance and delicate finish of Correggio, the almost divine creations of Raphael and the morning glories and sunset splendors of Titian. Ezekiel, however, in some of his poetic raptures reminds the lover of art of the wild passion and stern grandeur of Michael Angelo.

We will but briefly refer to the productions of the Minor Prophets who lived before the Captivity. They are called minor prophets on account of the brevity and not the inferiority of their writings. With the exception of Jonah they were all poets. Most of them were men of intellect and considerable culture for their age. Bishop Lowth says that even the prophet from the sheepfolds, in sublimity and magnificence of conception, and in splendor of diction was not inferior to any of his brethren. Their range of vision in the fields of prophecy was not as extensive as that of Isaiah, but what they saw was vivid and magnificent, and their genius was kindled into a beaming glow. They seem to have spoken very little to mankind, but they spake with tongues of fire in

"Thoughts that breathe and words that burn."

Nahum deserves a separate and more particular reference, as he was a poet of very high order. His ardent patriotism seems to have added vigor, boldness and sublimity to his genius, and elevated his strains. His "burden of Nineveh" is luminous with splendid imagery and rings out like a rapturous triumphal song in accompaniment to the silver trumpets of Israel.

We cannot pass in silence the book of Habakkuk, especially his ode, which seems to condense in a short compass the excellence and glory of prophetic poetry.

From the realms of nature and the various sources of human feeling he seems to have extracted the very essence of poetry, and given it utterance in language of varied forms, grand then tender, sublime then beautiful, majestic then simple, stern and strong, and then flowing in liquid and brilliant harmonies.

The Prophets of the Restoration had clear and bright hopes of the long expected Messiah, but they had none of the sublime spirit of poetry. Their light was like the ruddy glow on the evening cloud when the sun has set, and the twilight is gathering in thickening gloom over the valleys and the hills. Some of the sweet and plaintive Psalms are supposed to have been written after the Captivity. The Old Hebrew lyre had hung so long upon the willows of Babylon and sighed in the restless winds that its loftiest chords were broken, and when the few lingering delicate strings were touched by loving hands they only breathed forth subdued and weeping melodies, where once they had sounded with sublime and glorious rhapsodies.

How could Judah sing the songs of pride and rejoicing under circumstances of such deep sadness. A little remnant of old Israel had returned from long and painful captivity and servitude to their fatherland, desolated by the tread of the stranger and full of rude and hostile aliens. Ten of the tribes had been scattered in the distant East to return no more, and half of Judah and Benjamin had remained in the homes of the conquerors. The exiles had forgotten their sacred and noble language and could only utter the harsh and rugged accents of the Aramaic tongue. The Ark of the Covenant was gone; the light of the Shechinah shone no more above the mercy seat, the Urim was silent and the celestial fire no longer blazed upon the brazen altar. No wonder the priests, Levites and old men wept as they stood beside the foundations of the new temple and remembered Zion in her former glory.

We will not enter into the history of the post-exillian period although it is full of events of importance and of thrilling interest. We have rejoiced too long amidst the light and beauty of the free intellectual and poetic life of the Old Hebrews to follow their descendants into their condition of sadness, degeneracy and gloom. The cohesiveness of the race was greatly lessened, and thousands of Jews voluntarily sought homes in the crowded marts of Alexandria, Antioch and other cities of the Mediterranean. The people became divided into various religious sects; everywhere local synagogues furnished convenient places of worship, and thus was greatly weakened the vivifying influence of the temple service; and the peace of the feeble and tottering State was often disturbed by internal dissensions and civil wars. The Jews were in the midst of the strifes and convulsions of surrounding nations, and were often swept over by the angry and desolating tides of conflict, and yet they maintained their peculiar civil and religious institutions for more than five hundred years when, as a nation they were completely overwhelmed and dispersed by the relentless power of Rome. But the light of their genius was not quenched, and the seeds of their civilization were carried on the currents of time to all lands, where they germinated and added to the rich, moral and intellectual harvests of succeeding ages. The Jewish state has been appropriately and vividly compared to a ship—mastless and rudderless, "tossed in the trough of the sea," its destruction continually threatened by the surging billows, and at last completely overwhelmed and its rich cargo scattered with the fragments of the wreck on the wild waves to be carried by currents and the restless winds, and stranded upon every island and every shore.

The saddest but not least instructive chapters in history are those which record the declension and downfall of nations. The existence of nations has often been compared to the changing periods of a day. Nations have the misty glories of the morning, the splendors of the noontide and the varying hues of the setting sun, then they melt into the gloaming of the twilight and some darken into the almost impenetrable gloom of the oblivious midnight.

The life of Greece was a brilliant day illumined with the light of genius and cultivated taste, and although her national power has passed away, still the golden glories of her intellectual sun-light beam in an after-glow of radiant beauty round her tomb.

The long and eventful life history of Rome was a day of military power and intellectual achievements and had the sublimity and splendors of the storm, and was closed with the fierce tempests of Gothic invasion, which was followed by the murky darkness of the Middle Ages.

The day of Hebrew national life dawned in mild and quiet beauty among the hills of Palestine and shed its celestial brightness amidst shifting shadows and varying clouds for more than ten centuries, and then the gloomy hours of the evening began with the Babylonish Captivity, and then for four hundred years came the deep brooding twilight, when a new sun rose upon the dark rim of the horizon to begin a new day that will never close in night, but continue to brighten the moral and intellectual world, carrying light, life and joy unto all the races of men, until it blends with the effulgent and eternal day of Heaven.

The poetry of the Hebrews sprang from the soul of their free national and religious life, and when they became captives and slaves they seemed not to have breathed its highest inspirations. But the notes of majestic and pathetic harmony which once sounded from the Old Hebrew lyre is as immortal as the music of the spheres, and has swelled through the centuries of the past, and elevated and ennobled human thought in every age, and thrilled with joy and hope the hearts of mankind.

LECTURE XV.

SOME OF THE CHARACTERISTICS OF HEBREW POETRY.

In this lecture I propose to refer again to some of the characteristics of Hebrew poetry, to which I have heretofore only briefly and incidentally alluded.

I will not enter into the intricate mazes of theology or attempt to expound and interpret the profound oracles of divine truth. Neither will I present many quotations of beautiful phrases and verses from the Bible. I will not make selections of jewels of thought from the rich casket which you all have in your homes. I will not give you cups of sparkling water, when you can so readily refresh and invigorate your minds and hearts by drinking at the living fountains.

An obvious characteristic of Hebrew poetry is concentration of thought. In it we find no elaborate discussion of a theme, no minute description of a scene. It often repeats and amplifies a sentiment in different words, but the language is always sententious and glowing. The illumination which it throws upon many obscure subjects is like the quick and vivid flashes of the lightning at night which for a moment reveal every object in the range of vision with the intensity of electric light. Many of the natural objects thus revealed by the lightning are at once recognized and comprehended by the beholder, while others are like shadowy phantoms, vanishing in succeeding gloom, which the clear and steady light of the ensuing day discloses as real objects of utility and beauty.

Thus there are many truths by the Hebrew bards which when first uttered found their way to the minds and hearts of the hearers, while others seemed grand and shadowy and inspired feelings of indefinable reverence and awe. Many of these old mysteries have been cleared away by the revelations and teachings of the Gospel and by the events of succeeding ages. We feel well assured that the time will come when every page and verse of Moses and the Prophets will glow with the clear light of truth and with immortal beauty to the believing mind and pious heart as they did to the fervid hearts of Cleopas and his companion as they walked and talked with the risen Christ on the way to Emmaus.

There are verses in the Bible which seem to be concentrated expressions of thought and feeling, never losing or diminishing in vividness and beauty. Many of these verses have furnished materials and suggestions for numerous songs, poems and sermons, and still they have not been exhausted of their rich and abounding fullness. Like the widow's cruse of oil and handful of meal they ever furnish the bread of life.

Hebrew poetry has a wonderful power and facility of adapting itself to the mental and moral capacities of all classes of men and to every condition of life. While it furnishes rich thoughts, sublime imagery and profound wisdom to the highest and most cultivated intellect, it also whispers consolation and joy to the ignorant and the lowly. It is like the sunshine which not only enters the carved casements of palaces and the stained windows of gorgeous cathedrals, but also pours its joyous and inspiring light and warmth over the wild and solitary landscape and through the cracks of the cottage, and everywhere spreads beauty, fertility and gladness. We can account for this universality of influence in Hebrew poetry in no other way than by believing that it is animated by the spirit of an all-wise, beneficent and omnipotent Creator.

Any one at all familiar with the literary productions of Christian nations will be forcibly struck with the penetrating and permeating power of Hebrew thought and language. You can scarcely read any book which teaches moral and physical truths which does not contain apt and forcible quotations and illustrations from the Old Testament. Even in works of fiction some of their most brilliant passages are tinged with the coloring of the old Hebrew mind. We find the gems of Hebrew thought and language giving force and beauty to grand orations which electrified Senates and forums or sounded from the tribune and roused the enthusiasm of the people and controlled the destinies of States. In all the intercourse of social, public and domestic life we continually hear or use passages from the Old Testament which point an argument, illustrate a proposition, call up some sweet memory, brighten some hope, purify some affection and elevate our noblest emotions. There are many verses in the Bible which like seraph voices seem to pervade the intellectual and moral world. Many of these verses are in themselves complete poems, and when recited alone teach important moral and spiritual truths, and although these various verses may be upon different subjects there exists between them the most perfect harmony. We may not be familiar with all these little poems, but when we first hear them we have no difficulty in recognizing them as parts of the Bible, as they all breathe its divine spirit. They are like certain sea-shells which anywhere and everywhere will murmur the music of their ocean home. There are many golden texts of scripture which linger in our hearts like strains of unforgotten melody and are associated with loved accents heard no more on earth but which, we believe, are mingling with the choirs of Heaven. Day by day, and year by year, we may gather these pearls and golden grains of divine truth and lay them up in the treasuries of mind and heart, but as we grow holier and wiser, we will feel like the great father of modern astronomy when he said " I have picked up a few pebbles on the strand, but the ocean is still to explore."

One of the highest evidences of the power and excellency of poetry, is the influence which it has had in hallowing and immortalizing the scenes, events and localities to which it has referred. The proud towers of Ilium were prostrated in the dust and the remnants of the nation scattered in exile over the earth, before the periods of authentic history but the Iliad and Æneid have given the heroes of Troy and its mound of ruins a classic immortality. Athens and republican and imperial Rome still live in the eloquence and songs of their children, and have received the veneration of twenty centuries. Scott and Burns have thrown around their rugged country a halo of rhythmic glory and made Scotland dear to the hearts of the civilized world. They have made her old kirks and ruined castles, her placid lakes and shadowy glens; her flowery braes and misty moorlands, her heathery hills and rude highlands—"haunted and holy ground;" while her rushing streams, wimpling burns and singing birds seem ever repeating the melodies of her matchless bards.

The intelligent tourist as he passes along the castled Rhine or gazes upon the cloud capped Alps feels his imagination glowing with the inspiration with which poetry has enchanted the beauty and grandeur of nature. The pride and power of Venice have passed away, the fame of her Doges has been forgotten, stately argosies fill not her marts with the wealth and luxury of every clime, and her costly palaces no longer gleam in magnificence and resound with strains of festal joy, but poetry and art have wreathed her brow with fadeless *immortelles* as in poverty and decay she rests in indolent repose on the bosom of her bridegroom sea, and dreams only of her former glories. I might refer to numerous other facts for the purpose of showing the hallowing and immortalizing influence of poetry, but they will readily suggest themselves to your minds so familiar with the history of literature.

If we judge the writings of the Old and New Testaments by this standard of excellence we will find that they far exceed all the productions of human genius. They have immortalized every land to which they have referred. They have kept ancient Nineveh, Babylon and Tyre from the graves of oblivion, and thrown a hallowing charm over Egypt and the Nile, over the desolate mountains and barren sands of Arabia, over the ruins of Palmyra and the gardens of Damascus.

The ruthless Roman destroyed the temple of Zion, levelled the walls of Jerusalem, and the persecuted remnants of Israel have been scattered like dust before the whirlwind; and for eighteen hundred years Palestine has been the Aceldama of nations; the home of poverty, suffering and sorrow, of injustice, ignorance and oppression; but still it is the Holy Land, sacred to Mohammedan, Jew and Christian, and the names of its towns and cities, its hills and vales, mountains and plains, rivers and seas, groves and fountains are dear familiar household words in every clime where the Bible has been read, honored and loved.

Another striking characteristic of Hebrew literature, to which I have already incidentally alluded, is, its marked and distinctive individuality, which is, in a great degree, preserved even in its translation into other languages. A German book translated into English may readily be mistaken by the general reader as the production of an English mind. An accomplished philologist may be able to discern some shades of thought or some idiomatic expressions peculiar to the *faderland*, but in the general mass of literature the book loses its individuality. It is not so with the Bible. No philological research and acuteness are required to detect Bible thought and language. They may be introduced into every species of literature and give it force and beauty, but they never so completely commingle as to lose their characteristic identity. Bible expressions require no quotation marks to distinguish them. The Hebrew style of thought and expression always remain as peculiar and distinct among literatures as the Hebrew race among other peoples.

The Jews mingle among all other peoples and yet they preserve a personal identity which distinguishes them as the seed of Abraham. With the exception of parts of the books of Ezra and Daniel, which were written in Chaldee, there is a wonderful similitude of thought and modes of expression among the writers of the Old Testament which were preserved for more than a thousand years through all of the eventful periods of Hebrew history. Some of the writers were more highly gifted than others in inspiration and natural genius, and the style of some was more elegant and rhythmical than that of others, but there were very few dialectical differences in the construction of the language, and the vocabulary was not much enlarged and enriched. The written language seems to have been developed in force and vigor from the time it was first used by Moses and Job. In the times of David and Solomon it was somewhat improved in elegance and refinement by the superior genius of those princes and the master-singers of the temple—Asaph, Heman and Jeduthan—and in the age of the later prophets it manifested some feebleness and decline, but during its existence as a living language it remained unchanged in its essential elements. The reasons which produced this similitude of style and preserved the language from material changes must be obvious to all persons familiar with Hebrew history and the distinctive characteristics of the people.

This unchangeableness of language and modes of thought does not exist in the same degree in any other national literature. The writings of Chauser differ from the productions of Tennyson, and the literatures of the intervening periods distinctly show a dissimilarity of thought and language, and are filled with the peculiar characteristics of the several ages in which they were written. The people in those several ages differed as widely in manners and customs as in their literatures. It was not so with the Hebrews. The Hebrews of the exodus, in most respects, were like the Hebrews who went into Captivity. Among the Jews of the present day, dwelling in every land, there is a striking physical and moral resemblance. A true personal description of a Jew of the Middle Ages would suit the Jew of the nineteenth century, and we have reasons for believing that in either age he was in many respects similar to the people who followed Joshua into Canaan.

The Bedouins of the desert have retained the marked peculiarities of the sons of Ishmael for four thousand years and the same destiny has been accorded to the Isaaic descendants of Abraham. The Ishmaelites, dwelling amidst the fastnesses and dreary desolation of the desert, were inaccessible to the revolutionary influences of surrounding nations; but the Jews have been among all people, passed through the countless revolutions of decades of centuries, and while most of the other ancient races have been commingled, by conquests and other causes, and formed into new peoples, the Jews have preserved their national peculiarities. Thus the books of the Old Testament, which have been translated into so many different languages and been scattered over the whole earth, are the same in substance and spirit as when read before the Tabernacle, in the temples of Solomon, of Zerubbabel and of Herod, and in the Churches of Christendom for eighteen hundred revolutionary centuries. God has preserved His Word with the same care, that He has preserved the identity of his Works.

The Heavenly hosts that poured the glory of their primal light over Eden, and upon which the Chaldean Magi gazed in reverent worship, have ever kept their unvarying orbits and shone with their unchanging splendors. Thus His Word to His spiritual Israel of every age and every race is the same in substance and spirit as that which He spoke to His chosen people whom He so long guarded and blessed in the Holy Land.

In the literary structure of the Old Testament there are commingled human and divine elements which specially adapt it for purposes of instruction and guidance to mankind. The Bible is the inspired Word of God, written by holy men; but the language in which it is written is human speech, and the symbols, metaphors and illustrations used by the authors were derived from history, from the events of ordinary life and from familiar natural objects. We cannot disintegrate this mysterious combination of divinity and humanity, and separate by any accurate analysis these different elements. God has joined them in harmonious union and man cannot put them asunder. We know the combination exists, that it was effected by the Holy Spirit and was intended for wise and beneficent purposes.

The incarnation of our Saviour and His love, sympathy and sorrow for man and His constant practice of the beautiful human virtues make Him so dear and lovely to the Christian heart, "God manifest in the flesh" is a sublime mystery, which not even the angels comprehend, but still this inscrutable mystery is full of consolation, joy and hope to all believers.

We cannot understand the Trinity in Unity which we believe to exist in the Godhead. We cannot tell how the spiritual, moral, mental and physical natures of man are commingled into the great and harmonious problem of life. We cannot fathom the mysterious purposes and providences of God as He controls the destinies of men and nations. There are thousands of mysterious combinations of different elements in the economy of nature which we do not, and never can understand, and yet we recognize their existence and experience their beneficence, and feel that they are the works of God. The Bible has many sublime mysteries which we cannot solve, but it is so full of pictures of human life accurately delineated, and it contains so many blessed truths that impress themselves with living power upon our minds and hearts, and which are so fully sustained by our observation and experience, that we receive these mysteries with strong and holy faith and heed all the teachings as the Word of God. We cannot reasonably expect the finite mind to grasp the infinitude of God and fully comprehend Him in His word or in His works as He controls the illimitable universe by plans and purposes which exist from the eternity of the past and through the eternity of the future.

There is an immortal vitality and power in the Bible which has preserved it through every danger and will make it completely triumphant over every obstacle. Those who fear that its influence will be overcome by human error have somewhat the timid spirit of the Spies who dreaded the earthly power of the sons of Anak, when the everlasting arms and sheltering wings of Jehovah were around and above His people Israel. When we know what wonderful achievements the Bible has already made, and what difficulties and dangers it has already successfully encountered, why should we have doubts as to its future progress, when so many increased facilities for its rapid advancement and diffusion are daily brought into operation by an overruling Providence? God has manifested His goodness and power in every period of history—His shining footprints are on all the sands of time, and shall we fear that He will desert His people in their future progress and suffer the influences of His Word to be overcome by the powers of darkness. His word is clothed with the immortal armor of divine truth and can never be destroyed.

We have a strong and abiding faith in the continued progress of intellectual, moral and spiritual development. We concur in none of the gloomy forebodings of those who would induce us to believe that our Christian civilization will retrograde and may some day become extinct. The history of the world shows that all the changes and revolutions of the past have been but preparatory for future events. Age has been linked to age, and in the struggles between good and evil which have existed in all times we can trace the slow but gradual development of God's moral government. There have been many dark eddies in the stream of human progress, but they seem to have added force and volume to the current in its onward flow, and is like a great river which grows broader, deeper and more majestic as it approaches the sea. If the governments and institutions of the ancient world have been destroyed we can readily understand the causes which produced such results. The civilizations of the ancient nations—with the exception of the Hebrews—were founded in systems of force, wrong and oppression. Their governments were built up and sustained by the sword and they perished by the sword. Their social institutions were structures built upon the sand and have been swept away by the floods of time.

These ancient systems of civilization acted and reacted upon each other, overturning empires and forming out of their ruins new political organizations, which were again subverted by disasters until absolute despotism over all mankind was established in the Roman Empire—the embodiment of violence, injustice and oppression—and from the dark deluge which overwhelmed this gigantic power sprang the modern world.

We will not attempt even a sketch of the long conflict

between ancient and Christian civilizations. Both seemed to be engulfed in the barbarism of the Middle Ages, but they were not completely destroyed. They both came forth purified from the terrible ordeal, and all the elements of ancient civilization worth preserving now adorn and give vigor to human advancement. The Reformation enunciated the higher and purer spiritual doctrines of Christianity and also the great and divine truths of civil, intellectual and religious freedom, which in some nations have been firmly established and in others they are still struggling with sure hopes of ultimate triumph.

The principles of Christian civilization are derived from God's word, and they will endure as long as the everlasting hills which God has placed upon the granite foundations of the earth. The human mind has been emancipated by divine truth and can never again be enslaved, but will continually advance in enlightenment and power. Force, ignorance, injustice and oppression may still for a time darken the destiny of the human race, but they will pass away before the continually increasing influences of Christian civilization.

In looking back over the history of human progress we have seen the misty, then ruddy twilight of the dawn, we have seen the Sun of Righteousness rising amidst the lurid storms of the morning, slowly scattering the dark clouds and lulling the fierce winds, and now we can look with the calm confidence of faith upon the more tranquil azure of advancing day, and may we not hope that our posterity will, at no distant age, dwell amidst the brightness of the unclouded noon.

LECTURE XVI.

THE UNINSPIRED POETRY OF THE HEBREWS. THE JEWS IN HISTORY. THEIR RETURN TO THE HOLY LAND.

In preceding lectures we have very briefly and imperfectly considered some of the characteristics of Hebrew literature. We fully believe that the Bible, written by the Hebrews and their Jewish descendants, is the primal source of true statesmanship and every wise system of laws. It is the Magna Charta of human liberty and the great peace-maker among men and nations. It binds society together by the ties of social charities and the kindly feelings of brotherhood. It kindles and keeps active the fires of love on the home altars and fills the sorrowing heart with hope and joy. It is the chief teacher of refined and elegant culture and the repository of the most pathetic and sublime poetry, and has exerted the highest influence upon the advancement of the civilization of mankind.

Although the Old Testament is so full of inestimable truths, so rich in thought and wisdom and so much adorned with eloquence and poetry, we can but regret that the entire mass of Hebrew literature has not come down to our age. We have sufficient evidence for believing that the Old Testament contains but a small portion of the rich, extensive and varied literature of the Hebrews that once cultivated the minds and enriched the thoughts and imaginations of the early oriental nations. We cannot be surprised at the scarcity of the literary remains of this ancient people when we remember that oblivion rests upon so much of the literatures of other nations of a subsequent age who were more closely connected with the history of modern times. We possess comparatively few of the productions of Grecian and Roman genius. The fable of the Sibyl seems to represent the fate of ancient literature, of which only a few precious volumes have been left for the instruction and delight of mankind. The rude hands of the Vandal and Goth not only overturned many of the palaces and temples of ancient Rome, but also destroyed a large portion of the treasures of ancient learning, art and poetry. We are informed that the Alexandrian library contained seven hundred thousand volumes, which the torch of Omar scattered in ashes over the desert. In every literature there were thousands of the productions of the human mind which exerted a beneficent influence in their age which have been lost forever in the whelming tides of time.

We may well believe that a people as highly intellectual and imaginative as the Hebrews, with such a rich store of legendary memorials, and surrounded by so many influences which have produced poetic inspirations in other nations, must have had many odes and songs commemorative of past history, legends and traditions that existed among them during the period of their national life.

Where are the thousand and five songs which Solomon wrote? Where are many of the sublime utterances of Elijah and Elisha and other prophets who guided and instructed Israel? The "Schools of the Prophets" were schools of poetry, music and polite learning, and must have produced many songs and poems of the highest excellence. Where are the simple and soothing lullabies of childhood, the joyous epithalamiums of the marriage feast and the sweet harmonies of the happy home? Where are the plaintive elegies with which affection consecrated the graves of the loved and lost? Where are the cheering songs of the vintage and harvest home, and the soul stirring odes with which patriotism celebrated the triumphs of national valor?

The simple shepherd must have carolled many a sweet pastoral song as he sat beneath the fig-tree or spreading vine and watched the sportive gambols of the lambs of his flock and the lambs of his household upon the beauteous greensward near the crystal fountain.

The ardent Hebrew lover must have sung many a soul stirring lyric as he wooed the warm-hearted daughter of Shem; and the silence of the hazy twilight must often have been broken by the tender lays of the dark-eyed maiden of Israel, as like a nightengale, she breathed the minstrelsy of love upon the balmy breezes as they kissed the cheeks of the sleeping flowers.

Our regrets for the loss of the uninspired poetry of the Hebrews are in vain. It must have contained many beautiful gems, which have gone down to the deep unfathomable caves of the deluge of time. Only the poetry that was vitalized by the spirit of divine inspiration has, like an ark, moved in safety amidst the wrecks and drifts of time over the stormy billows of the ages.

The word and works of God are alike indestructible by force or time. We know that many of the objects in the material world are subject to disintegration and decay, but science informs us that not the smallest particle of matter has ever been annihilated. God has told us that not one jot or tittle of his word should fail. That word has been translated into various languages and although it may have thus lost to us some of the original literary elegancies with which it was adorned, it still teaches the loftiest truth and wisdom in language of wondrous melody and beauty, and touches the same sweet chords in the human heart which it touched three thousand years ago, and makes them thrill with glorious harmonies.

Man and time may change some of the features of nature, and form natural elements into new combinations, but they cannot dim the brightness of the sun, or turn the shining planets from their orbits; they cannot control the swelling tides of the ocean, or remove from their deep foundations the everlasting hills. Thus the word of God will endure forever, have free course and be glorified in fulfilling its divine mission. God has preserved as much of the history and literature of the chosen people as was necessary for the guidance and instruction of mankind, and this record will remain unchangeable and indestructible. He has also wonderfully preserved the identity of His chosen people.

Their history is eventful, peculiar and full of sadness. They forgot the sacred covenant, rejected and crucified their Messiah, and their beautiful house was brought to desolation—not one stone left upon another—and for more than eighteen centuries they have been outcasts and exiles from the land of their fathers and their sacred and ruined altars.

> "The wild dove hath her nest, the fox his cave,
> Mankind their country, Israel but the grave."

The story of the Wandering Jew is a fit representation of the destiny of the race. It is said that he offered indignities to Christ while on the way to Calvary and was cursed with an immortality of wandering and suffering. He is represented in the legend as visiting every part of the earth in his endless pilgrimage; always weary but never resting; mingling in society without receiving any of its love, comforts or blessings; passing unharmed through torrid heat and arctic winter; through the storms of the ocean and the dangers of the land; through the carnage of battle-fields, the blazing ruins of sacked cities, and the charnel houses of the pestilence, always seeking destruction but never destroyed; he seems to have had nothing of life but the anguish of suffering, and all of death but the rest and quietude of the grave.

Thus the Jews, since the destruction of their Holy City, have been outcasts and wanderers. They are found in all periods of history mingling with other races and always remaining a separate and peculiar people. They are to be found in every clime, and the tireless foot of the Jew has trod every shore. They have been succesful in collecting the riches of commerce and controlling the finances of the world. They have entered every grade in society from the hovel of the peasant to the palaces of nobles and kings. They have led conquering armies, and with thrilling eloquence commanded the applause of listening senates, and as powers behind the throne, have directed victorious legions and controlled the jurisprudence and diplomacy of States. They have guided the advancing march of civilization and have ever been the earnest advocates of social order, freedom and justice.

During the supremacy of the Moors in Spain, the Jews for eight centuries found a home and protection in that land of sunny skies, fertile plains and vine-clad hills, almost as beautiful as their motherland; and by their talent, learning, industry and energy greatly assisted in building up a civilization in the splendid cities of Andalusia whose intellectual light and glory have scarcely yet been excelled in human progress. But the time for their permanent rest from wandering and freedom from persecution had not yet come. The bigotry and fanaticism of Ferdinand and Isabella drove them from their new Palestine and scattered them again amongst the nations, and a gloom of ignorance, superstition and despotism settled upon that devoted land which has not yet been dispersed by the glowing light of modern civilization.

The sacred books of the Hebrews, which contain but a portion of the learning, wisdom and genius of the race, have given religions, laws and the highest literatures to the civilized nations of the world. They have given vitality, cohesiveness and power to Islam and much of the elevating, enlightening and civilizing spirit of Christianity. In all the noble contests of the human mind against prejudice, oppression and wrong, and in the progressive advancement of mankind towards enlightenment, truth, freedom, justice and right, their sacred books have led the vanguard, even as the pillar of cloud and fire led the wanderings of their forefathers through the wilderness to the Promised Land.

The history of four thousand years shows the Hebrews to be not only the oldest but one of the noblest and most enduring races of men. In all the departments of learning and intellectual effort, in creative genius and cultivated taste they have stood as peers with the most gifted of the sons of men. They have won some of the richest trophies in the fields of science and philosophy, added invaluable treasures to literature, beautified the noblest galleries of art, and thrilled the hearts of mankind with strains of the loftiest melody.

There is something sublime in the spiritual solitude of the Jew. He mingles freely in all species of business, and sometimes enters into familiar social intercourse, but still there is a *penetralia* in his heart to which no Gentile influence can obtain access. There he enshrines the tenets of his religious faith and the enduring love of his fatherland, clustered round with memories and hopes which are undimmed by disappointments and unshaken by disasters; and how earnestly and continuously does his heart breathe the prayer of the Psalmist,

"Oh! that the salvation of Israel were come out of Zion; when the Lord bringeth back the captivity of His people, Jacob shall rejoice and Israel be glad."

"Do good in thy good pleasure unto Zion, build thou the walls of Jerusalem."

What natural principles and elements could have produced such a national phenomenon as the Jews, having no parallel in history. God does nothing without some purpose and "He hath not dealt so with any nation." He is fulfilling the sublime prophecy which He spoke more than three thousand years ago through the unwilling lips of Balaam.

> "Lo, the people shall dwell alone
> And shall not be reckoned among the nations."

He has preserved this remarkable people in their distinctive character and nationality to accomplish some great end in the future. The Jews are as numerous now as the Hebrews were when Joshua led them into Canaan. Among all nations they are remarkable for their thrift, industry and commercial energy, and for them the streams of trade seem to flow over golden sands. They have generously cared for their indigent people, and the name of a Jew is never found on the lists of pauperism. They generally practice the virtues of temperance and chastity and observe most of the duties of citizenship.

When we consider the insults, vexations, wrongs and oppressions which they have endured; the cruelties and calamities which they have suffered; the scorn, contumely and contempt which have been heaped upon them in every age of modern times, by Pagan, Moslem and Christian, by serf, freemen and king, we cannot be surprised that many of them have exhibited the vices of avarice, hypocracy, cunning and deceit. These vices were learned by the Jews in the schools of their bitter experiences as the only means of self-preservation and protection, and we are surprised that in passing through such a terrible ordeal they have preserved so many of the human virtues. Until a recent period they have scarcely found a land that afforded them a secure home and the equal benefits of its laws, and could they be expected to love a country in which they were oppressed and regarded as aliens and outlaws? They have scarcely ever mingled with a people who extended to them the sympathies of human brotherhood, or the courtesies and amenities of ordinary social intercourse, and could they reasonably be expected to exhibit the highest social virtues and charities in return for distrust, scorn and reproach? Has the conduct of Christian nations in their continual strifes and revolutions—deluging the earth with all the sins and sorrows of war—been well calculated to inspire the Jew with admiration for our Christian institutions, and give him confidence in our sincerity and reverence for the religion which we profess, and which teaches as a primal doctrine, "On earth peace, good will toward men?"

The unparalleled problem presented in the social, political and intellectual condition of the Jews can be solved in no other rational way than by attributing the highest principles of conservatism to their religious faith, and by supposing that still, for some wise and beneficent purpose, The Lord of Hosts is with them, the God of Jacob is their refuge.

The dark and cruel prejudices of eighteen hundred years are passing away before the advancing light of a purer and holier Christianity and a nobler civilization, and the political skies of the Jews are brightening around them. In most civilized countries they are no longer subjected to tortures and oppressions, but receive the protection and benefits of the laws; and in England and in the United States they enjoy as much freedom as their ancestors did in the palmy days of the Hebrew common-wealth. Profane history furnishes no information by which we can account for the long preserved and distinctive existence of the Jews, and it fails to afford any light in forecasting their religious and political future. On this subject we must look to the books of prophecy and the blessed promises of the Gospel of the Prince of Peace, God alone can solve the mysterious problem of Jewish life.

As God in His corrective providences has dealt sorely with the Jews, so He has dealt with the beautiful land which He gave to their fathers as a habitation and inheritance. Both the people and their land are witnesses of the curse of the broken covenant, of Jehovah's righteous judgments and of the truths of divine prophecy.

Once this land was garnished with all the lavish bounties of nature and was filled with abundance, but now it is barren like a desert, and her beauty and fertility have been trodden down by oppressors and strangers. Once it teemed with a free, intelligent, industrious and prosperous population whose homes were flourishing hamlets, ancient towns and splendid cities, but now it is sparsely inhabited by slothful peasants, decrepid beggars, dejected slaves and vicious robbers, dwelling in miserable villages in filth and poverty. Its cities are wasted and its sanctuaries brought to desolation—it is a field of rubbish and ruins. How truly has the prophecy been fulfilled: "Your country is desolate, your cities are burned with fire, your land strangers devour it in your presence, and it is desolate as overthrown by strangers." "And the daughter of Zion is left as a cottage in a vineyard, as a lodge in a garden of cucumbers, as a besieged city."

As God has kept the Jews in all ages and in the midst of all nations a separate and peculiar people, so has He kept the land which He gave their fathers from being the distinctive home of any other nationality. It was overrun by the Chaldeans, Assyrians, Egyptians, Persians, Greeks and Romans, and in succeeding ages by still greater destroyers, the Arabians, Saracens, Crusaders, Mamelukes, Tartars and Turks, but to none of these nations and races has it been a permanent and prosperous home. Palestine seems to have ever been conscious of and responded to the undying love of her exiled and scattered children; and for centuries in dust and ashes she has mourned for their absence, their sorrows and misfortunes.

Since her bereavement she has put off her beautiful garments and clothed herself in the habiliments of sorrow and woe. Her breezes are no longer balmy with their former delicious perfumes and she smiles no more in fresh and dewy verdure. Many of her gushing springs, musical rills and singing birds are silent, and many of the beauteous wild flowers that bloomed on her bosom have faded. The stately forests that once crowned her mountains with regal pride and glory, and the fruitful fig trees, olives and vines that mantled her hillsides have been trodden down by the Gentiles; and golden harvests no longer wave in her valleys and over her plains ready to fill storehouses of plenty. The sound of tabret, viol and harp are not heard in festive homes and the voices of rejoicing are all at rest. Her once crowded highways are desolate and her now barren fields are not covered with flocks and herds, and resound not with the blithesome songs of the vintage and harvest. Once with maternal fondness she lavished rich blessings upon her children, and now that they are gone she refuses to bestow bounties upon the oppressors and heedless strangers. She will put on her glorious apparel no more or yield her hidden treasures until the set time to favor Zion shall come, and the outcasts of Israel and the dispersed of Judah shall be gathered into the dwellings of Jacob.

The restoration of the Jews to the Holy Land is distinctly foretold in prophecy, but the time of its accomplishment is known only to God. We fully believe that the Jews will in some coming age recognize the Messiah promised unto their fathers, and with pride and holy joy will acknowledge the truth of the superscription placed by the infamous Pilate in mockery on the Cross, "Jesus of Nazareth, the King of the Jews," and will see the truth and beauty of the prophecy: He shall be "a light to lighten the Gentiles and the glory of Thy people Israel.

When that grand event shall occur then the time of the Gentiles will be fulfilled, "And the ransomed of the Lord shall return and come to Zion with songs and everlasting joy upon their heads, they shall obtain joy and gladness and sorrow, and sighing shall flee away." They shall come from the four corners of the earth and from the islands of the sea and be gathered into the land long since promised unto Abraham and his seed forever, and there show forth the praises of the Lord.

"The wilderness and the solitary place shall be glad for them, and the desert shall rejoice and blossom as the rose." "It shall blossom abundantly and rejoice with joy and singing; the glory of Lebanon shall be given unto it—the excellency of Carmel and Sharon; they shall see the glory of the Lord and the excellency of our God."

Then all the blue mountains of Israel shall put off their garments of desolation—be crowned with garlands of vines, fruits and flowers, and grow green with pastures. The hills on every side shall be covered with flocks and herds, and shall flow with milk and honey, and the valleys become fat with wine and oil and abundant harvests. The fountains and streams and birds and trees and breezes, with songs of rejoicing, will join in the glorious jubilate that welcomes the return of the redeemed exiles of Israel to the "goodly land" of Promise. Then the waste places of Jerusalem shall be built up, the place of the sanctuary shall be beautified, and the place of His feet be made glorious, and again shall she be "beautiful for situation, the joy of the whole earth." Then the daughters of Zion shall arise from the dust and put on their beautiful garments and have beauty for ashes, the oil of joy for mourning and the garment of praise for the spirit of heaviness. Then the poets of Israel will wake again the long, silent Hebrew lyre to sing in the lofty strains of Christian millennial joy, the fulfilment of those divine promises and purposes which the Old Hebrew Bards saw in the glorious visions of prophecy three thousand years ago.

GREENSBORO
LAW SCHOOL.

The Sessions will commence on the First Monday in January and Third Monday in August, and terminate the Second Monday in June and December.

TUITION.

$80.00 for entire course, or $50.00 per session, to be arranged in advance.

There will be six examinations and lectures each week.

Board can be obtained in private families at from $12.00 to $16.00 per month.

COURSE OF STUDY.

Blackstone's Commentaries (2d book) diligently.

Coke, Cruise, or some other standard work on Real Property.

Stephen and Chitty on Pleading.

Adams' Equity and 1st Greenleaf on Evidence.

Some standard work on Executors and Administrators

Code of Civil Procedure.

ROBERT P. DICK.

www.ingramcontent.com/pod-product-compliance
Lightning Source LLC
Chambersburg PA
CBHW020909230426
43666CB00008B/1369